Why Bother with Elections?

Why Bother with Elections?

Adam Przeworski

polity

First published in 2018 by Polity Press
Reprinted: 2018, 2019, 2020

Polity Press
65 Bridge Street
Cambridge CB2 1UR, UK

Polity Press
101 Station Landing, Suite 300
Medford, MA 02155, USA

ISBN-13: 978-1-5095-2659-8
ISBN-13: 978-1-5095-2660-4(pb)

A catalogue record for this book is available from the British Library.

Library of Congress Cataloging-in-Publication Data

Names: Przeworski, Adam, author.
Title: Why bother with elections? / Adam Przeworski.
Description: Cambridge, UK ; Medford, MA, USA : Polity Press, [2018] |
   Includes bibliographical references and index.
Identifiers: LCCN 2017023458 (print) | LCCN 2017052210 (ebook) | ISBN
   9781509526628 (Mobi) | ISBN 9781509526635 (Epub) | ISBN 9781509526598
   (hardback) | ISBN 9781509526604 (pbk.)
Subjects: LCSH: Elections. | Politics, Practical. | Political culture. |
   Representative government and representation.
Classification: LCC JF1001 (ebook) | LCC JF1001 .P78 2018 (print) | DDC
   324.6--dc23
LC record available at https://lccn.loc.gov/2017023458

Typeset in 10.75/14 Adobe Janson by
Servis Filmsetting Ltd, Stockport, Cheshire
Printed and bound in in the United States by LSC Communications

For further information on Polity, visit our website: politybooks.com

Contents

Figures

Preface

This book is a summary of our current collective understanding of the method by which some societies decide who would govern them and how: elections. While I rely heavily on my own research, I draw extensively on work of others. Because the book is intended to be accessible to the general educated public, I dispose with the usual academic etiquette, which consists of acknowledging the source of every idea and every fact. I decided to provide sources of direct quotes but not to reference the origins of other inspirations. Hence, I owe an apology to those of my colleagues who will recognize themselves as authors of ideas anonymously presented below.

"Collective understanding" does not mean that scholars studying elections agree on everything. I try to report differences of views and beliefs, as well as aspects of elections about which we are not clear, but I am certain that some people will still disagree with some of what follows. Hence, the reader is urged to read this book critically, forming opinions of his or her own.

For comments on earlier drafts I owe gratitude to John Dunn, Roberto Gargarella, Fernando Limongi, Zhaotian Luo, Bernard Manin, Pasquale Pasquino, and Ruben Ruíz-Rufino, as well as to three anonymous reviewers.

I

Introduction

We select our governments through elections. Parties propose policies and present candidates, we vote, someone is declared winner according to pre-established rules, the winner moves into the government office and the loser goes home. Glitches do sometimes occur but mostly the process works smoothly. We are governed for a few years and then have a chance to decide whether to retain the incumbents or throw the rascals out. All of this is so routine that we take it for granted.

As familiar as this experience is, elections are a perplexing phenomenon. In a typical election about one in two voters ends up on the losing side. In presidential systems the winner rarely receives much more than 50 percent of the vote and in parliamentary multi-party systems the largest share is rarely higher than 40 percent. Moreover, many people who voted for the winners are dismayed with their performance in office. So most of us are left disappointed, either with the outcome or with the performance of the winner. Yet, election after election, most of us hope that our favorite candidate will win the next time around and will not disappoint. Hope and disappointment, disappointment and hope: something is strange. The only analogy I can think of is sport: my soccer team, Arsenal, has not won the championship in many years but every new season I still hope it will. After all, in other realms of life we adjust our expectations on the basis of past experience. But not in elections. The siren song of elections is just irresistible. Is it irrational?

Questions concerning the value of elections as a mechanism by which we collectively choose who will govern us and how they will do it have become particularly urgent in the last few years. In many democracies large numbers of people feel that elections only perpetuate the rule of "establishment," "elites," or even "caste" ("*casta*" in the language of the Spanish *Podemos* party), while at the other extreme many are alarmed by the rise of "populist," xenophobic, repressive, and often racist, parties. These attitudes are intensely held on both sides, generating deep divisions, "polarization," and are interpreted by various pundits as a "crisis of democracy" or at least as a sign of dissatisfaction with the very institution of elections. Survey results show that people in general and young people in particular now consider it less "essential" than in the past to live in a country that is governed democratically – all of which supports the claim that democracy is in crisis (Foa and Mounk 2016).

Yet there is nothing "undemocratic" about the electoral victory of Donald Trump or the rise of anti-establishment parties in Europe. It is even more paradoxical to claim the same about results of various referendums, whether about Brexit or about constitutional reform (but implicitly Europe) in Italy: referendums are supposed to be an instrument of "direct democracy," regarded by some as superior to representative democracy. Moreover, while the label of "fascist" is carelessly brandished to stigmatize these political forces, such parties, unlike those of the 1930s, do not advocate replacing elections by some other way of selecting rulers. They may be seen as ugly – most people view racism and xenophobia as ugly – but these parties do campaign under the slogan of returning to "the people" the power usurped by elites, which they see as strengthening democracy. In the words of a Trump advertisement: "Our movement is about replacing a failed and corrupt political establishment with a new government controlled by you, the American people" (<https://www.youtube.com/watch?v=vST61W4bGm8>). Marine Le Pen promised to call for a referendum on Europe, in which "you, the people, will decide." They are not anti-democratic. Moreover, there is nothing anti-democratic about people wanting to have a "strong" or "competent and effective" government – responses to survey questions, which have increased in frequency during recent years and which some commentators interpret as a symptom of declining support for democracy. Schumpeter (1942) certainly wanted governments to be able to govern and to govern competently, and I do not see why other democrats would not.

Dissatisfaction with the results of elections is not the same as dissatisfactions with elections as a mechanism of collective decision-making. True, finding oneself on the losing side is disagreeable. Surveys do show that satisfaction with democracy is higher among those who voted for the winners rather than the losers. Moreover, having been offered a choice, the fact that parties presented distinct platforms in the electoral campaign is valued by the winners more than by the losers. But what people value most in elections is just being able to vote for a party that represents their views, even when they end up on the losing side (based on Harding's 2011 study of 40 surveys in 38 countries between 2001 and 2006). When people react against "the establishment," they often just mean either that no party represents their views or that governments change without an effect on their lives, indicating that elections do not generate change. But we can, and a large majority does, value the mechanism of elections even when we do not like their outcomes.

Why should and why do we value elections as a method for selecting by whom and how we wish to be be governed? What are their virtues, their weaknesses, and their limitations? My purpose is to examine such questions, taking elections as they realistically are, with all their blemishes and warts, and to distill their effects on various aspects of our collective well-being. I argue below that some popular criticisms of elections – specifically that they offer no choice and that individual electoral participation is ineffective – are mistaken, based on an incorrect understanding of elections as a mechanism by which we decide as a collectivity. I contend that, in societies in which people have different interests and divergent values, looking for rationality (or "justice") is futile, but that elections provide an instruction to governments to minimize the dissatisfaction with how we are governed. Whether governments follow these instructions ("responsiveness") and whether elections serve to remove governments that do not ("accountability") is more questionable: governments that are egregious are subject to electoral sanctions but their margin to escape responsibility is large. I fear that the perennial expectation for elections to have the effect of reducing economic inequality is tenuous in societies in which productive property is held only by a few and in which markets unequally distribute incomes – "capitalism." The greatest value of elections, for me by itself sufficient to cherish them, is that at least under some conditions they allow us to process in relative liberty and civic peace whatever conflicts arise in society, that they prevent violence.

This is a minimalist, "Churchillian," perspective, a view that admits that elections are not pretty, that they are never quite "fair," that they are impotent against some barriers they face in particular societies, and that they are far from realizing the ideals that led to their emergence and are still held by some people as the criteria to evaluate them. But no other method of selecting our rulers, I believe, can do better. No political system can make everyone's political participation individually effective. No political system can make governments perfect agents of citizens. No political system can generate and maintain in modern societies the degree of economic equality that many people in these societies would like to prevail. And while maintaining civic order and non-interference in private lives never cohere easily, no other political system comes even close. Politics, in any form or fashion, has limits in shaping and transforming societies. This is just a fact of life. I believe that it is important to know these limits, so as not to criticize elections for not achieving what no political arrangements can achieve. But this is not a call for complacency. Recognizing limits serves to direct our efforts toward these limits, elucidates directions for reforms that are feasible. Although I am far from certain to have correctly identified what the limits are, and although I realize that many reforms are not undertaken because they threaten interests, I believe that knowing both the limits and the possibilities is a useful guide to political action. For, in the end, elections are but a framework within which somewhat equal, somewhat effective, and somewhat free people can struggle peacefully to improve the world according to their different visions, values, and interests.

Obviously, when examining what is good, bad, or inconsequential about elections, a natural question is "compared to what?" Rulers were traditionally selected by the rules of heredity, in contemporary China they are selected by the incumbents, and in many places around the world they still impose themselves by only thinly veiled force. Different methods of selecting rulers occur under different conditions, so if we were to consider just the observed world we would not be able to distinguish effects of the historical conditions from the effects of these methods. To make comparisons, we would have to ask counterfactual questions: what would have transpired in the United States if governments were not elected or what would have transpired in China if they were? Such comparisons between observed and counterfactual states of affairs can be and are routinely made but they are based on all kinds of assumptions, which leave a lot of discretion and tend to generate inconclusive results. I do not pursue this path systematically but return to the importance of realizing that all political institutions, elections included, function in particular societies, variously divided by income, religion, ethnicity, or whatever else, and that there are limits to what any government, elected or not, can achieve.

What I am after is the difference elections make when they are competitive, when they offer a real choice of governments, when people can remove incumbents and choose their successors if they so wish.[1] Hence, I am asking about the effects of "democratic" elections, as contrasted with all

---

[1] A technical comment (I promise the only one) to make it clear what I mean by "competitive" elections. Suppose that the rules say that someone (person or party) wins an election having obtained at least proportion v^* of the vote. Now suppose that a proportion v^I is certain to vote for the incumbent and a proportion v^O for the opposition, while we do not know how the remaining proportion will vote. The probability that the incumbent will win is then

$$p = \frac{v^* - v^O}{1 - v^I - v^O}$$

so that if $v^*=0.5$, $v^I=0.45$, and $v^O=0.40$, $p=2/3$. The closer is this probability is to 0.5, the more competitive the election will be. Note that the probability of winning is not the same as the margin of victory: if one party is *certain* to win v^*+1 *vote*, the probability is 1. Elections are competitive if *ex ante* their results are uncertain, not when the margin of victory turned out to be small *ex post*.

other methods of selecting rulers, whether they hold elections which they are certain to win or not hold them at all. But, to answer this question, we need first to understand why elections would or would not be competitive, and why the incumbent rulers would place their power at stake in elections.

Competitive elections – again, elections in which those in power lose when a majority of voters so wish – are no more than a speck in human history. The use of force – coups and civil wars – has been frequent and still continues to erupt in poor countries: between 1788 and 2008 political power changed hands as a result of 544 elections and 577 coups. The very idea of selecting governments by elections is quite recent and still quite rare. The first national-level election based on individual suffrage, in which representatives were chosen for a limited term, dates only from 1788; the first time in history that the helm of the government changed as a result of an election was in 1801; both events took place in the United States. Since then people across the globe have voted in about 3,000 national-level elections. Yet electoral defeats of those in power were rare until very recently and peaceful changes of governments even less frequent: only one in about five national elections resulted in defeats of incumbents and even fewer in a peaceful change in office. Still, as of 2008, 68 countries, including the two behemoths, China and Russia, had never experienced a change in office between parties as a result of an election.

Hence, voting need not mean electing. The mere fact that an event called an "election" is held does not necessarily mean that people have a choice of selecting their rulers. Indeed, some such events, elections in one-party systems, were intended to persuade the potential opposition that it has no chance to remove the rulers by any means, aiming to intimidate rather than to select. In many other countries, elections are contested but not competitive: some opposition is legally allowed but the incumbent rulers make sure that no one has a chance to remove them. Yet, even if elections do not decide who will rule, it does not mean that they are irrelevant or even unimportant. Those who see such elections as mere "window dressing" must ask themselves why some rulers, say those in Russia, care to dress their windows, while others, as is still true in Saudi Arabia, do not bother to do it. Holding non-competitive elections is a trick, but it is based on the ideal that the ultimate source of power resides in the people, with recognition of the norm that people have the right to be governed by governments they choose. Admitting a norm and violating it in practice is a tenuous undertaking. Hence, even when they are not competitive, one element that all elections have in common is that they make all rulers nervous. Moreover, even non-competitive elections may reduce civic violence by revealing information about the rulers' relative military strength, and thus about the probable failure of any attempts to remove the ruler by force.

Why would elections not be competitive? One reason is that losing elections is not only unpleasant but can be dangerous to entrenched elites. Even when the idea that political representation must be based on elections became irresistible, founders of representative governments feared that equal political rights exercised through elections would threaten property. They reasoned that if everyone has an equal right to influence political decisions and if a majority of the people is poor, that majority would vote to confiscate property. Systems of representative government were born under a fear of participation by the broad masses. One would not err much in thinking that the strategic problem of "founders," pretty much everywhere, was how to construct representative government for the rich while protecting it from the poor.

This divergence between ideology and reality set up a particular dynamic of conflicts that have continued over 200 years and persist today. The successive trenches by which property was defended from majority rule – repression of opposition, non-elected upper chambers, the right of non-elected powers to veto legislation, restrictions on the eligibility to be elected, restrictions on the right to vote, open voting, indirect voting – had to be overcome one by one. And when these bulwarks were demolished, new ones were erected to protect property from the outcomes of elections: validating laws became increasingly placed in the hands of non-elected justices, while control over monetary policy was shifted to non-elected central banks. The relation between property and power has been the axis organizing political conflicts over the past 200 years, with outcomes varying across periods and countries. It cannot be solved once and for all.

The second reason is that elections are a threat not only to economic and social privilege; they can be personally threatening to the holders of political power, which is when they use all the instruments at their disposal to avoid electoral defeats. It matters what the stakes in an election are, *what* one would lose, not only *whether* one would lose. When incumbents fear that an electoral defeat may mean a loss of life, freedom, or even just fortune, the risk is just too high to be tolerated. Put yourself in the of place of President Putin. The opposition does not just want to defeat but to destroy him: it accuses him of breaking laws, of amassing a fortune, even of having bombed a Moscow building as a pretext to intensify the Chechen war. His risk of losing is likely to cause some foreboding. Hence, many rulers hold rituals which they call "elections," but see to it that they do not lose. Elections in which incumbents expose themselves to the possibility of defeat are possible only if the incumbents believe that their opponents would reciprocate if they become the rulers. Losing is always unpleasant, but if all that losing entails is that you would continue to live comfortably while waiting for your chance in the next election, this risk is tolerable. Elections are competitive – incumbents expose themselves to the possibility of losing – only when their stakes in the outcomes of elections are not too high, when all that is at play is who would govern for some fixed period of time, perhaps promoting the interests of those who elected them but not threatening vital interests or values of those who opposed them.

When they are truly competitive, elections are a mechanism by which we, as a collectivity, decide who will govern us and how. Moreover, when they are regularly repeated, they give us a chance to express our dissatisfaction with the way we are governed. But what can we reasonably expect of elections in the real world, in which only some people enjoy the privilege of property, in which markets unequally distribute incomes, and in which parties and politicians do their utmost to perpetuate their political power? What follows is first a history of some aspects of elections: the very idea of electing governments, the perennial conflicts between majority rule and protection of property, and the evolving methods by which electoral incumbents protect their power. My purpose in reporting this history is to distinguish those features of the electoral mechanism that evolved over time and varied across countries from those aspects that are inherent in any election. Then, in the second part, I take elections at their best, when they are truly competitive, and study questions about their effects for selected aspects of societal welfare. I conclude by discussing the relation between elections and democracy.

Part I

HOW ELECTIONS WORK

2

The Idea of Electing
Governments

Why Elections?

Elections are a modern phenomenon. During most human
history, the right to rule did not require authorization from
those ruled. This right was taken to be natural, given by
the order of things or the will of some supreme authority.
The idea that "the people," always in the singular, should
govern itself was only ushered in at the end of the eighteenth century, as a result of two revolutions – in the United
States and in France. The problem to be solved, as posed by
Jean-Jacques Rousseau in 1762, was to "find a form of association which defends and protects with all the shared force the
person and the goods of each associate, and through which
each, uniting with all, still obeys but himself, remaining as
free as before" (Rousseau 1964 [1762]: 182). The solution
to this problem was "self-government of the people." Self-
government, in turn, was desirable because it was the best

system to advance liberty. We are free when we are bound only by laws we choose: this is the source of the power and appeal of "self-government."

Yet all cannot govern at the same time. We must be ruled by others. And ruling inevitably entails coercion. The rulers can take money from some and give it to others; they can force everyone to have needles stuck in their arms; they can keep people in jails, and in barbarian countries even take lives. Here then is the conundrum: how can people be free if they are coerced by others? The answer was that we can choose who would rule us by selecting them through elections. They would represent us because we elect them to do so.

The English king represented the nation just because he was the king. In France, Louis XVI doggedly resisted becoming the king of the French people: his mandate was of the king of France, independent of the will of anyone but God. Monarchs were neither delegates nor agents of the people. Still at the eve of independence in the United States, "election was incidental to representation; it was not supposed to be its source. The mutuality of interests between the representatives and those for whom they spoke was the proper measure of representation" (Wood 1969: 96).

The view that "mutuality of interest" is sufficient for representation never died. Carl Schmitt, an influential German twentieth-century political philosopher, claimed that the rule of the people is sustained whenever rulers act in the common good of everyone, regardless of how they are selected. The "essence" of democracy, etymologically the rule of the people, is "the identity of the dominating and the dominated, of the government and the governed, of he who commands and he who obeys" (Schmitt 1993 [1928]: 372), not elections. Yet this view opens room for any ruler to assert that he is "identical" with those whom he manipulates, oppresses, imprisons, and even kills. It allows rhetorical maneuvers, such as "the Russian political system – in its essence although not in form – does not differ in anything from real, serious Western democracies" (Russian journalist Mikhail Leontiev, in an interview with a Polish newspaper, *Dziennik*, January 19, 2008). The unity of the leader and the led is the "essence," while particular institutions, including elections, are just "forms."

The founders of representative government thought that only elections could ensure that the interests and values of rulers would coincide with those of the ruled. Already by the 1780s, elections had become the sole criterion of representation: as a member of the Constitutional Convention, James Wilson, put it, "the right of representing is conferred by the act of electing." The debate in revolutionary France focused on the veto power of the king. The question was whether the unelected king could be considered to be a representative of the nation. Abbé Sieyès, the ideologue of the French Revolution, took the electoral view of representation: "One should ask if the possibility of forming the common will that may become law can be confided to others than men elected for a term by the people. It is obvious that it cannot (*Il saute aux yeux que non)*" (Sieyès, quoted in Pasquino 1998: 92). Sieyès view was to prevail two years later: as Robespierre would say, "Without elections, no representation."

The principle that only those who were elected could be considered as representing the people was revolutionary. Not everyone found this solution satisfactory: Rousseau famously viewed it as self-inflicted slavery. Yet it took a short time before the right to govern became based exclusively on elections. The relation between representation and elections took root because it was motivated by the principle that if the people constitute the only source of power, the people must authorize any exercise of power over them. The people may not be the best judges of what is best for them – "it may well happen that the public voice, pronounced by the representatives of the people, will be more consonant to the public good than if pronounced by the people themselves, convened for the purpose" (Madison, *Federalist* #57) – but to govern on behalf of the people, one had to serve at the bequest of the people.

It is controversial whether the idea of authorization also entailed the prospect of de-authorization. One argument was that if elections brought to office men distinguished by reason and virtue, ex-post control over their actions would not be necessary. Moreover, governments were to be controlled by other mechanisms: separation of powers, checks, and balances. Not everyone was equally confident, however, that the elected representatives would not abuse their power against the people, that they would not turn into "political aristocracy." Anti-Federalists feared that "Corruption and tyranny would be rampant as they have always been when those who exercised power felt little connection with the people. This would be true, moreover, for elected representatives, as well as for kings and nobles and bishops. . . ." Yet the very fact that elections were to be periodic meant that the authorization was temporary and that it could be withdrawn, that it was conditional.

Elections are the second best: although none of us can claim to rule oneself, collectively we can choose who will rule us. Moreover, if we do not like our rulers, we can periodically show our distaste by throwing them out. True, individual people must bow to the will of others: given heterogeneous preferences, some people must live at least some of the time under governments they do not like. Still, the collective power of the people to choose governments through the procedure of elections renders sufficient plausibility to the belief that the will of the people is the ultimate arbiter of rule. We consent to being coerced – we could not live together peacefully unless we are coerced – because we can decide who should exercise coercion and how. People are free because they can choose their rulers.

The Spread of Elections

Once the idea appeared on the historical horizon, the spread of elections was vertiginous. The first national Congress was elected in the newly formed United States of America in 1788. Revolutionary France and the short-lived Republic of Batavia (Netherlands) held elections still before 1800, the Spanish Empire celebrated the election to the Junta Central in 1809, Norway in 1814, Portugal in 1820, the newly independent Greece in 1823, while Belgium and Luxembourg followed in 1831. All Latin American countries, beginning with Paraguay in 1814, had joined this list by 1848. Liberia held elections in 1847. The revolutionary years of 1848–9 witnessed the first elections in the Austrian and Hungarian parts of the Empire, in the Netherlands and in Denmark. Including Britain and the Caribbean British colonies, by 1850 at least 31 independent countries or dependent territories had an experience of voting in at least one legislative election. By 1900, this number was 43. Most countries that emerged from World War I had elected legislatures at least during a part of the inter-war period, when first elections were also held in several dependent territories. During the first few decades of the twenty-first century, all but a handful of countries have legislatures elected by universal suffrage and chief executives either elected in popular elections or indirectly by elected parliaments.

Figure 2.1 shows the proportion of the observed units (independent countries or dependencies; their number is shown by shaded bars and counted on the left scale) that held elections in each year. Note that the average constitutional term of presidents or legislatures is 4.6 years, which means that if elections were held regularly, they should have occurred each year in about 22 percent of countries.

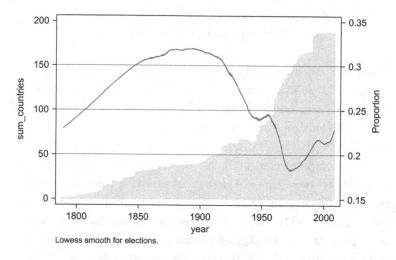

Lowess smooth for elections.

Figure 2.1 *Proportion of countries holding elections, by year*

The change was epochal. Countries that got rid of distant monarchs replaced them with elected chief executives, presidents. The remaining monarchies gradually adopted constitutions that provided for lower houses of legislatures to be elected on the basis of individual suffrage, with the right to convoke themselves, and to control the purse. The idea of electing one's rulers was thus obviously captivating. The change was both sudden and momentous, revolutionary. Indeed, it was frequently ushered in by revolutions.

The Myth of Self-Government through Elections

At every moment of political life of every society, some people rule over other people, issuing commands and enforcing them by the threat or the actual use of force. This fact is inevitable. At most it can be masqueraded. Indeed, if people are to believe that they rule themselves when they elect others to rule them, it must be masqueraded. The plausibility of this belief is not given once and for all. As Morgan (1988: 82) observed, "The problem of reconciling the wishes and needs and rights of actual people with the overriding will of a fictional sovereign people was not temporary. It was, indeed, inherent in the new fiction."

Elections are supposed to convey instructions to those elected to do what citizens would have done themselves in their place. According to Henry Peter, Lord Brougham, "the essence of Representation is that the power of the people should be parted with, and given over, for a limited period, to a deputy chosen by the people, and that he should perform that part in the government which, *but for this transfer*, would have been performed by the people themselves" (quoted by Pitkin 1967: 150). Another eighteenth-century writer thought that "a full and equal representation is that which possesses the same interest, feeling, opinions and views the people themselves would were they all assembled" (Richard Henry Lee, quoted by Herreros 2005: 18). Representation, in Madison's view (*Federalist* #52), is "a substitute for the meeting of citizens in persons."

But this transfer is not innocuous. Even if representatives were a random sample of the people, they would acquire distinct interests and specific information as representatives. They need not even be selfish; they may just need to make compromises in order to adopt policies desired by their constituents. Yet the constituents still cannot be certain whether the compromises that have been reached are the best possible for them. It is possible that all the elected representatives want is to act in the best interest of the people as a whole – which is what Edmund Burke in 1774 thought they should be doing: "Parliament is not a congress of ambassadors from different and hostile interests, which interests each must maintain, as an agent and advocate, against other interests and advocates;

but Parliament is a deliberative assembly of one nation, with one interest, that of a whole. . . ." But even if they do this, and act as trustees of what they see as the common interest, nothing guarantees that this would be the interest their constituents wanted them to pursue.

In fact, for reasons discussed below, representatives are never a random sample of the people. They are individuals distinguished by some traits, with their own interests, values, and beliefs. The ideological revolution introduced by elections was more profound than the real one. Representative government meant, for the founders, government of those endowed with reason and virtue, but reason and virtue were reserved to those distinguished by wealth, gender, and race. While governments were to be selected by elections, elections merely ratified the superiority of those qualified to govern by their social and economic position. The poor were instructed that their interests are represented by the wealthy, women that their interests are guarded by men, the "uncivilized" that they need to be guided by their colonizers. Self-government, equality, and liberty were dressed up in elaborate intellectual constructions to make them compatible with rule by a few. Created under a shadow of religious and economic conflicts, representative institutions were designed to bar or at least minimize the voice of the people between elections, treating all "intermediate organizations" – clubs, associations, and trade unions, as well as political parties – as a danger to civil peace. Intended as a bulwark against despotism, representative institutions were designed to disable governments from doing much of anything, bad or good, by checking and balancing powers, by protecting the status quo from the will of the majority.

The benevolent guise of paternalism, whether extended to the poor, women, or people who were not "civilized," was a veneer covering interests. And the veneer was thin: it wore off as soon as it touched on property. The relation between property and power was intimate and often unabashed. This is why some voices are so revealing: they only bare the true beliefs, real intentions. The people cannot be trusted because it can "err": James Madison said it, Simón Bolvar said it, and so did Henry Kissinger. And the gravest error people could commit was to use political rights in a quest for social and economic equality, to associate in pursuit of higher wages, decent working conditions, material security, to encroach on "property." Even when the poorer classes could no longer be excluded, a plethora of inventive devices neutralized the effects of their political rights. As one speaker observed in the Spanish parliamentary debate about universal suffrage in 1889, "We are going to establish universal suffrage, and then what is going to happen in our national political history? Nothing. . . ." Naked force stood as the ultimate bulwark against threats to property. But institutional systems often provided sufficiently effective trenches.

The plausibility of the belief that elections express active consent of free individuals obviously depends on whether people have a real chance to choose governments, most importantly, whether they are able to remove the incumbent rulers by the act of voting. But what also matters are the stakes in elections, their consequences for the policies of the elected governments. As the Italian political philosopher, Norberto Bobbio (1989: 157), observed, "to pass a judgement today on the development of democracy in a given country the question must be asked, not 'Who votes?' but 'On what issues can one vote?'" When the status quo, whatever it is, is protected from the majority by all kinds of institutional trenches, the belief that people can decide in elections not only who rules but also how they would rule is undermined.

To be credible, the ideology must at times exercise causal power over reality: institutions must be reformed so as to maintain this credibility. This is how Morgan (1988, all quotes from pages 13–14) interpreted the origins of self-government in England and the United States in a masterful essay ironically entitled *Inventing the People*. "Government requires make-believe," Morgan observes. "Make believe that the king is divine, make believe that he can do no wrong or make believe that the voice of the people is the voice of God. Make believe that the people *have* a voice or make believe that the representatives of the people *are* the people." But an ideology is plausible only if it corresponds to something in real-life experience: "In order to be effective, . . . a fiction must bear some resemblance to fact." Most of the time we adjust fictions to facts. But at times facts must be adjusted to fictions. Fictions can cause facts: "Because fictions are necessary, because we cannot live without them, we often take pains to prevent their collapse by moving facts closer to fit the fiction, by making our world conform more closely to what we want it to be . . . the fiction takes command and reshapes reality." And this implies, to finish the quotes, that "In the strange commingling of political make-believe and reality the governing few no less than the governed many may find themselves limited – we may even say reformed – by the fictions on which their authority depends."

Some extensions of political rights to those previously excluded and some reforms designed to make these rights effective occurred only in response to revolutionary threats: in this sense they were conquered by the insurgent masses. In turn, some reforms were granted by elites voluntarily, in their own interest, as historical conditions evolved. Another way to see this distinction is that some reforms make the elite worse off than they are under the status quo, even though better off than if the threat of revolution materialized, while other reforms make the elite or at least a majority thereof better off than under the status quo.

It is not always easy to tell which reforms constituted conquests but a peculiar aspect of these conflicts is that those who struggled for reforms justified their demands in terms of the ideals proclaimed by those against whom they fought. Working-class leaders pleaded for socialism in terms of equality and self-government: French socialist leader Jean Jaurès (1971: 71) thought that "The triumph of socialism will not be a break with the French Revolution but the fulfillment of the French Revolution in new economic conditions," while the German socialist Eduard Bernstein (1961) saw in socialism simply democracy brought to its logical conclusion. The Declaration of the Rights of Woman and the Female Citizen, written in 1791 by Olympe de Gouges (aka Marie Gouze), simply changed the gender in the 1789 Declaration of the Rights of Man to apply the same principles to women. Leaders of national independence movements appealed to the values of the colonizers: "Declaration of Independence of Democratic Republic of Vietnam," written by Ho Chi Minh, began with quotes from the US Declaration of Independence and from the French Declaration of Rights. And Martin Luther King's dream was "deeply rooted in the American dream." "Now is the time," he demanded, "to make real the promises of democracy." The myth of self-government through elections is powerful.

Elections as Methods of Choosing Governments

Elections are a method of choosing governments by counting votes. But government positions to be filled differ depending on how political institutions are organized, with a standard distinction between parliamentary, presidential, and mixed (semi-presidential) systems. While in parliamentary systems the government is elected by the legislature and in

presidential systems by popular vote, the crux of the distinction is whether the executive can be removed by a vote of
the legislature. Systems in which the government cannot be
removed by the legislature are presidential; those in which it
can be are parliamentary (or, where the president is popularly
elected, mixed). Bear in mind that a parliamentary government need not be supported by a majority of the assembly;
it is sufficient that a majority does not vote to remove it, so
that governments supported by only a minority of legislators
can, and in some countries routinely do, survive in office. In
turn, as distinct from impeachment, which is also possible in
presidential systems, members of the parliament do not have
to offer any reasons for voting non-confidence in the government. Frivolous threats of impeachment, particularly during
the Bill Clinton presidency, led some observers to comment
that the United States was becoming "parliamentary," but the
parallel is false: parliaments can remove governments without
accusing them of anything, whether financial scandals or
marital infidelity, just because a majority of parliamentar-
ians so wishes. In contrast, in presidential systems the chief
executive is popularly elected for a fixed term and cannot
be removed by the congress during the term by procedures
other than censure or impeachment. Thus, in parliamentary
systems governments are formed in two steps: voters select
legislators and then legislators select the government. In
contrast, in presidential systems voters select the chief executive and the legislators separately and then the elected chief
executive forms his or her government, sometimes subject to
approval of individual members by the legislature.

The second major difference among elections are the
ways in which votes are aggregated to determine winners and
losers. In some presidential elections, the winner is whoever
obtains an even small plurality of votes; in some, if no candidate obtains a majority or a qualified plurality of votes, there

is a second round among the two candidates who obtained the largest shares of vote in the first round; in some, the rules are more complicated. The United States is the only system in which elections for president are indirect.

The rules that determine how the distribution of votes is transformed into the composition of a legislature are more varied and more consequential. The main distinction is between electoral systems in which a plurality winner is elected from each district – "single-member single-district first-past-the post" (SMD for short) – and systems in which more than one member is elected from each district according to some rule of proportionality (PR for short). Most countries use one or the other of these systems, but some combine them. These rules are consequential because they affect the number of political parties that compete in elections. The "Duverger law," after the French political scientist Maurice Duverger, held that countries that use SMD have two parties, while those with PR have several. More recent research documents that the effect of SMD depends on the structure of social and regional cleavages in the society, but there is little doubt that PR promotes multi-partism. The second consequential effect is that, given the number of parties, these rules generate different degrees of divergence between the shares of popular vote and of legislative seats of the parties. Suppose that, as in the United States, there are two parties in the SMD system: if one of the parties wins 50 percent plus 1 votes in 50 percent plus 1 districts and no votes in other districts, it will obtain a majority in the House of Representatives having won only 25 percent of popular vote. At the other extreme, a pro-portional representation system in which the entire country constitutes a single district, as in Israel or the Netherlands, requires a party to get 50 percent of popular vote to obtain 50 percent of legislative seats.

Which is better: single-member-single-district or

proportional representation systems, presidentialism or parliamentarism? Proportional representation has the obvious virtue of being more representative. It is more representative because it allows more different strains of public opinion to be heard in elections. In French elections, for example, distinct parties campaign in the first round to "stop globalization," "redistribute incomes," "give vote to foreigners in local elections," "allow hunting," or "expel immigrants." It is also more representative in the sense that it reduces the divergence between vote and seat shares or the frequency of "unearned majorities." Yet, while it is praiseworthy that everyone be represented, someone must govern. Because proportional representation promotes the existence of several parties, often the result of an election is that no single party has a majority in the legislature and either a majority coalition is formed with heterogeneous goals or a minority government (perhaps also a coalition) has to build legislative majorities for each piece of legislation it wants to pass. In turn, SMD tends to generate single-party majorities, "earned" or not, so there is a party that can govern in a stable way. This dilemma led several countries to combine proportional representation with some devices that increase the probability that some party would have legislative majority, from combining the two electoral systems, as in Germany, to an outright gift of the necessary seats to the party that wins a plurality of votes, as in Italy.

The issue of presidentialism versus parliamentarism is even more complex and highly controversial, in part because these systems may function differently in different combinations with an electoral system. Single-party legislative majorities tend to be somewhat more frequent in presidential systems and these majorities almost always support the independently elected presidents. "Divided government," in which a legislative majority opposes the president is almost exclusively a

United States specialty. Some scholars criticize parliamentary systems, which are typically accompanied by proportional representation, for the instability of their governments, with Weimar Germany typically cited as the bad omen. Yet what for some is "instability," for others is "flexibility." Presidential systems permit the continuation in office of governments that are highly unpopular, sometimes running in single-digit support ratings. Moreover, they admit situations of legislative paralysis, in which the legislature and the executive cannot agree on anything.

In sum, elections are not all the same. In different countries, people vote for different government positions and their votes are aggregated in different ways. This point should be remembered because the focus in what follows is on what all elections have in common, so that important differences among them are ignored unless they are relevant to a specific issue being discussed.

3

Protecting Property

In societies in which only some people enjoy property and in
which incomes are unequally distributed by markets, unfet-
tered majority rule presents a threat to economic privilege.
This observation was perhaps first enunciated by Henry
Ireton in the franchise debate at Putney in 1647: "It [universal
male suffrage] may come to destroy property thus. You may
have such men chosenor at least the major part of them, as
have no local or permanent interest. Why may not these men
vote against all property?" (quoted in Sharp 1998: 113–14).
It was echoed by a French conservative polemicist, J. Mallet
du Pan, who insisted in 1796 that legal equality must lead to
equality of wealth: "Do you wish a republic of equals amid the
inequalities which the public services, inheritances, marriage,
industry and commerce have introduced into society? You
will have to overthrow property" (quoted in Palmer 1964:

230). James Madison warned that "the danger to the holders of property can not be disguised, if they are undefended against a majority without property. Bodies of men are not less swayed by interest than individuals. . . . Hence, the liability of the rights of property. . . ." (*Federalist* #10).

Once coined, this syllogism has dominated the fears, as well as the hopes, attached to elections ever since. Conservatives agreed with socialists that elections, specifically universal suffrage, must undermine property. The Scottish philosopher James Mackintosh predicted in 1818 that "if the laborious classes gain franchise, a permanent animosity between opinion and property must be the consequence" (Collini, Winch, and Burrow 1983: 98). David Ricardo was prepared to extend suffrage only to "that part of them which cannot be supposed to have an interest in overturning the right to property" (Collini, Winch, and Burrow 1983: 107). Thomas Macaulay (1900: 263), in the 1842 speech on the Chartists, vividly summarized the danger presented by universal suffrage:

> The essence of the Charter is universal suffrage. If you withhold that, it matters not very much what else you grant. If you grant that, it matters not at all what else you withhold. If you grant that, the country is lost. . . . My firm conviction is that, in our country, universal suffrage is incompatible, not only with this or that form of government, and with everything for the sake of which government exists; that it is incompatible with property and that it is consequently incompatible with civilization.

The threat to property can be thwarted in all kinds of ways. If only those with property are elected, it is unlikely they would act against their own interests. If poor people cannot participate in electing, the majority of voters will not be poor. And even if both eligibility for office and suffrage are unrestricted, the people's voice can be "filtered and refined," as Madison had it, by public voting and indirect elections. Moreover, political institutions can be designed to make the majority required to alter the status quo not just 50 percent plus one, but an overwhelming majority. Finally, decisions that affect property rights can be subjected to the scrutiny of constitutional tribunals or delegated to independent central banks.

The trenches protecting property have been the subject of political conflicts over the past 200 years. As time went on, many were conquered. Perhaps most importantly, the right to vote was extended first to lower classes and then to women. The shift toward secret voting and direct elections freed the voice of majorities from social domination. The institutional evolution toward unicameral legislatures reduced the protection of the status quo. Yet the faith that reforms are cumulative and irreversible was and is repeatedly undermined by the inventiveness of the powerful in discovering new ways to protect their interests.

Who Can Be Elected?

Rulers are elected. But this does not mean that anyone can become a ruler. While the right to be elected was originally restricted to wealthy males, over time such legal restrictions have been abolished. But we continue to be governed by people unlike most of us. In no country does the composition of the governing bodies reflect the economic, gender, or ethnic composition of the population. Selecting people who are distinguished by specific traits is just inherent in elections.

Choosing rulers by elections is a recognition of an unequal capacity to govern. Manin's (1997) analysis of the counterfactual mechanism for selecting rulers – lottery – bares what he identifies as "the aristocratic nature of elections." If people were considered to be equally endowed with wisdom and virtue, and if their interests were harmonious, it would make no difference who rules: everyone would rule in the same way. And, if everyone were equal as a potential ruler, rulers could be chosen randomly from among the people. Even in a society ridden with conflicts, randomly selected people could rotate for short periods as the rulers and the ruled. As Manin amply documents, the idea of selecting rulers by lot was present on the intellectual horizon of the eighteenth century. Yet it was rejected in favor of a "chosen body of citizens, whose wisdom may best discern the true interest of their country, and whose patriotism and love of justice will be least likely to sacrifice it to temporary or partial considerations" (Madison, in *Federalist* #10). As Manin (1997: 94) observes, "Representative government was instituted in full awareness that elected representatives would and should be distinguished citizens, socially different from those who elected them."

Treating social status as an indicator of wisdom and virtue was manifest in early elections, when those "fit to govern" – a phrase still used by Winston Churchill in 1924 to disqualify the Labour government – were members of the propertied classes. This association eroded over time, in particular with the advent of mass working-class organizations. We now choose among competing candidates, organized in parties, proposing platforms and programs. Free elections mean that each voter can decide which qualities of the candidates are to be considered relevant, and that any observable indicator of these qualities can be applied according to personal preference. But we still recognize that some people are more qualified than others. As Dworkin (1996: 27) observes, "We certainly do want influence to be unequal in politics for other [than financial] reasons: we want those with better views or those who can argue more cogently to have more influence." To repeat after Manin (1997: 149), "election cannot, by its very nature, result in the selection of representatives who resemble their constituents." We choose our betters.

Moreover, politics has become a hierarchically organized profession. Young people enter it at the bottom, patiently climb the echelons, to become prominent politicians only with age. Most politicians we recognize have been around for a long time. Even when some of them circulate between the public and the private sector, they form a "political class." True, there are reasons we should want politics to be a profession: after all, like any other occupation, politics requires skills that can be acquired only at the job. But it is also true that people who have done little else in their life have little empathy for how the rest of us live.

Elections need not entail full freedom of entry and a full range of feasible outcomes. In fact, they never do. Every political system structures the ways in which social interests are organized as political actors, regulates the barriers of entry to politics, and constrains in a variety of ways the policy proposals that become subject to electoral competition.

All political systems regulate the conditions under which particular groups can compete in elections. All require registration of political parties, often imposing some conditions. In French presidential elections, for example, to become a candidate an individual must obtain support of at least 500 among roughly 80,000 officials elected at different levels of government. This condition is weak, but a former prime minister failed to obtain the requisite support in the 2012 elections. Many countries repress some political ideologies or some political organizations, selecting the political forces that are permitted to organize and compete. Even regimes generally considered as democracies sometimes ban forces considered as anti-democratic (communists in West

Germany, McCarthyism in the United States). In the United States, the most important barrier to entry is simply money: competing in elections requires privately mobilized financial resources.

All political systems also regulate public speech. Some directly censor the content, but censorship is not necessary to filter what is said in public. Private speech may be free, but public speech is inevitably costly; hence, it must be sponsored. It may be sponsored by taxpayers, it may be sponsored by private interests, but sponsored it must be. Even when academics such as myself are given an opportunity to speak in public, someone pays for the room, someone pays for my travel, someone pays for the research that gives me something to communicate. Political speech, speech intended to persuade others of something that may result in policies that would bind everyone, is thus the reserve of a few. How many people have ever spoken to an audience of more than a hundred? And, again, these few are not just anyone. They are professional politicians, public officials, journalists, religious leaders, academics, film-makers, and writers: in Manin's sense, "an aristocracy."

Hence, even when elections are free and competitive, in spite of all the transformations, this much is just inherent in the mechanism of elections. Today, as 200 years ago, not everyone can be authorized to rule and not everything can be proposed in public.

Who Can Do the Electing?

To prevent "the people" from erring, founders of representative institutions thought it wise to limit the people who would exercise the right to elect to wealthy males. As a result, the gap between universalist ideology and exclusive institutions was veiled only thinly. Even the French 1789 Declaration of Universal Rights of Man and Citizen qualified its recognition of equality in the sentence that immediately followed: "Men are born equal and remain free and equal in rights. Social distinctions may be founded only upon the general good." Arguments for excluding some people from the body of the people appear almost desperate, so convoluted that their self-serving quality is apparent. The gap was so stark that it undermined the credibility of popular rule and led to conflicts that in many countries lasted over a hundred years. Neither the poor nor women thought that their best interests were being represented by propertied men. They struggled for suffrage, and suffrage was seen as a dangerous weapon.

Consider the justification of this exclusion by Montesquieu (1995 [1748]: 155), who started from the principle that "All inequality under democracy should be derived from the nature of democracy and from the very principle of democracy." His example was that people who must work to live are not prepared for public office and would also have to neglect their functions. As barristers of Paris put it on the eve of the revolution, "Whatever respect one might wish to show for the rights of humanity in general, there is no denying the existence of a class of men who, by virtue of their education and the type of work to which their poverty had condemned them, is . . . incapable at the moment of participating fully in public affairs" (Crook 2002: 13) "In such cases," Montesquieu went on, "equality among citizens can be lifted in a democracy for the good of democracy. But it is only apparent equality which is lifted. . . ." (1995 [1748]: 155). The generic argument was that:

1 Representation is acting in the best interest of all.
2 To determine the best interest of all one needs reason and to implement it one needs virtue.

3 Reason and virtue have social determinants: not having to
   work for a living ("disinterest"), or not being employed or
   otherwise dependent on others ("independence").

In turn, the claim that only apparent equality is being violated
was built in three steps:

1 Acting in the best common interest considers everyone
   equally, so that everyone is equally represented.
2 The only quality that is being distinguished is the capacity
   to recognize and pursue the common good.
3 No one is barred from acquiring this quality, so that suffrage is potentially open to all.

When first elections took place – in England, the United
States, France, Spain, and the newly independent Latin
American republics – political rights were everywhere
restricted to wealthy males. In all these countries suffrage was
subsequently extended to poorer males and to women, while
the newly emerging countries tended to immediately grant
rights more broadly, so that political rights are now universal
in almost all countries that have any kind of elections. Yet
the road from representative government to mass democracy
took a long time to traverse. As of 1900, one country had
fully universal suffrage while 17 enfranchised all males. Only
during the second half of the twentieth century, more than
150 years after representative institutions were first established, did universal suffrage become an irresistible norm.
This evolution is portrayed in Figure 3.1.
    While the reasons for extending suffrage to poor males
may have differed from case to case, many extensions were
responses to the threat of revolution, or at least of popular
unrest. The classical explanation of extensions is that at some
point the excluded threatened to revolt and so, even if sharing

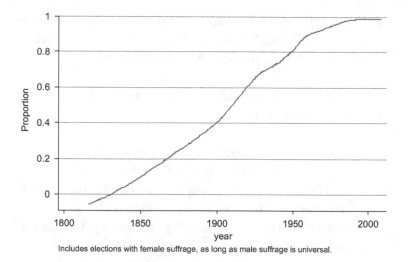

Includes elections with female suffrage, as long as male suffrage is universal.

Figure 3.1 *Proportion of elections with universal male suffrage*

political rights might have consequences that were costly for the incumbent elite, the elite preferrred to bear these costs rather than risk a revolution. A rival explanation is that some parts of the elite thought that extending suffrage would be in their interest, whether purely partisan or economic, so they reformed suffrage when they were in power.

Restrictions on female suffrage were motivated differently. While early proponents of female suffrage observed that reason is not distributed along gender lines, the main argument against giving the right to vote to women was that, like children, they were not independent and had no will of their own. Women were already represented by the males in their households and their interests were to be represented through a tutelary, rather than an electoral, connection. Thus the justifying criterion was dependence, not gender. Indeed, when a study in England in the 1880s discovered that almost half of adult women lived in households in which there was no adult male, this justification collapsed. The first country in which women could vote on the same basis as men in national elections was New Zealand in 1893, followed by Australia in 1902, Finland in 1907, and Norway in 1913. Between the two world wars female suffrage was adopted by 17 countries, including six newly independent ones. Yet still, as of 1945, only half of the countries with any kind of suffrage enfranchised women. With the proclamation by the United Nations in 1948 of the Universal Declarations of Human Rights, which banned all kinds of discrimination and asserted equality of rights between men and women, all but three Muslim countries – Bahrain, Kuwait, and Maldives – that became independent after this date extended suffrage to all men and women. Figure 3.2 summarizes this history, showing the number of countries in which women enjoyed suffrage on the same basis as men.

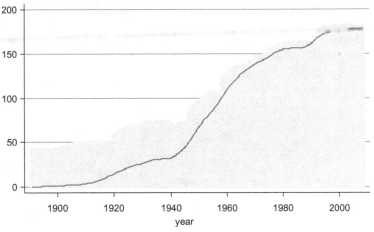

Lowess smooth. Bars show the total number of countries.

Figure 3.2 *Number of countries with equal women suffrage by year*

Filtering and Refining the People's Voice

Conceding rights did not mean conceding power. When the poor were allowed to vote, institutional devices regulated the consequences of their participation. The two devices through which the effect of political rights was typically controlled were indirect elections and public voting.

Indirect elections and restrictions of suffrage were used interchangeably: both were instruments to keep the majority of the population from exerting a direct influence on the composition of legislature. Scattered historical information indicates that indirect elections had a powerful effect in restricting representation by class. The indirectly elected French Convention was "an assembly of lawyers (52 percent of members) elected by peasants." One example of the effect of indirect elections comes from the 1847 elections in the Mexican state of Querétaro: while artisans and laborers con-

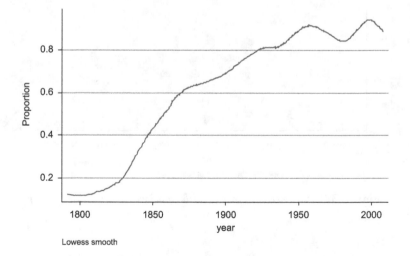

Lowess smooth

Figure 3.3 *Proportion of elections that were direct*

stituted 51.3 percent of the primary electorate and large landowners were few, the latter made up 58.3 percent of secondary electors and the former were completely absent among them. No wonder then that indirect elections were a powerful instrument protecting the incumbents. Incumbents lost 9.7 percent of 585 elections when elections were indirect and 23.5 percent of 2,113 direct elections. My calculations show that direct elections reduce the probability of an incumbent's victory by 13 percent.

Public voting, in turn, transforms relations of economic dependence into political dependence by intimidating poor voters, particularly in rural areas. As a Pennsylvania state legislator, Mark B. Cohen, once commented: "Open ballots are not truly free for those whose preferences defy the structures of power or friendship" (2005: <www.NationMaster.com>). If the electorate contains citizens who are not only unequal but embedded in relations of economic dependence, publicity of the electoral choice makes those who are dependent

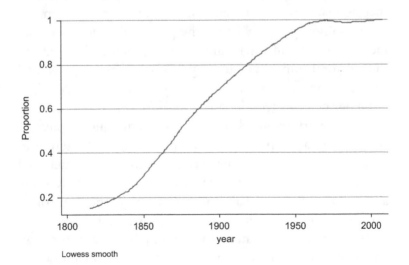

Lowess smooth

Figure 3.4 *Proportion of elections with secret voting, by year*

vulnerable to sanctions by their masters and thus exposes them to intimidation.

The effect of public voting on re-election chances is also large. Incumbents won 92 percent of the 449 elections in which voting was public and 76 percent of the 1,937 in which it was secret. Calculations show again that secret voting reduces the probability of an incumbent's victory by 13 percent.

Super-Majoritarian Institutions

Elections are a majoritarian mechanism: the winners are those who receive most votes. As Schumpeter (1942: 272–3) observed, "The principle of democracy merely means the reins of government should be handed to those who command more support than do any of the competing individuals or teams." Moreover, while sometimes a plurality share is sufficient to qualify for office, no electoral system requires more than a simple majority, 50 percent plus 1. And this rule means that as many as 50 percent minus 1 voters can be on the losing, minority, side. Hence, the perennial issue of democracy: what can and what cannot the electoral majority do to the electoral minority? How can the majority be prevented from abusing the minority?

One way to protect the minority is to increase the threshold of support required to alter any status quo: I refer to such devices as "super-majoritarian." The second is either to subject decisions of the majority to control by an unelected body, typically a constitutional tribunal, or to remove some aspects of policy, typically monetary, from the control of current majorities: such devices are "contra-majoritarian."

Any system of institutions which requires that more than one body must approve a particular law is super-majoritarian. Even when both the representatives and the presidents are elected by the same electorate, as long as they are elected according to different rules, each responds to a somewhat different majority and the result is that the effective majority required to pass legislation is more than just 50 percent. The president is elected at large by the entire country, the lower house is elected by districts, the upper house is typically elected by some sub-national units larger than the electoral districts. It is easy to see that as long as the majorities electing them are not identical, the result is a de facto supra-majoritarian threshold for altering the status quo, whatever it happens to be. If a bill must pass by a simple majority rule in two even slightly differently elected houses of the legislature, it may fail even if it would have passed by the same rule in the joint membership of these houses. The required supermajority may be quite high: according to some estimates, it is 75 percent in the contemporary United States. Figure 3.5 shows the evolution over time of the average size of legislatures. Most legislatures were bicameral during the nineteenth century but about half became unicameral after 1950.

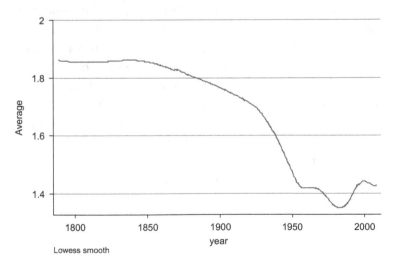

Figure 3.5 *Average number of houses of legislatures, by year*

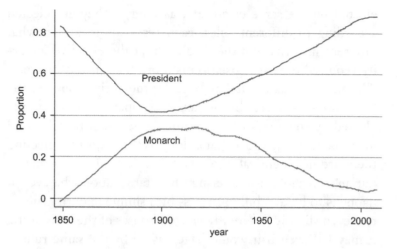

Figure 3.6 *Democracies in which someone can block legislation 1848–2008*

In turn, Figure 3.6 shows the proportion of democracies in which someone, either the monarch or an elected president (but not constitutional tribunals), could veto legislation adopted by elected legislatures. As we see, the frequency with which elected presidents had veto power declined during the second half of the nineteenth century but then continued to increase, while monarchs endowed with veto power became less frequent. Still, as of 2008, most countries had – directly or indirectly elected – presidents with at least suspensive veto power. Note that this figure portrays the constitutional prerogatives, not the actual use of the veto. British monarchs, for example, still have these powers but have not used them since the middle of the eighteenth century.

Counter-Majoritarian Institutions

In many democracies, even if a bicameral legislature passes a bill and the bill is not vetoed, the law can still be invalidated by a body which is not elected but selected by the elected representatives. The role of constitutional tribunals is to protect rights from whims of temporary majorities. This conflict between electoral majorities and constitutional courts is often portrayed as "democracy versus the rule of law." But law cannot rule; only people can. Law is not some impersonal force, acting as a logical machine. Whatever reasons they have, the law is what justices say it is. Both legislatures and courts are populated institutions. "Law rules" if governments elected by majorities listen to the court even if it rules against their constituency.

"Rights" are realms protected from outcomes of elections, entrenched by constitutional provisions that can be altered only by qualified majorities and specific procedures. Such constitutionally protected rights include civil and political liberties. But one should not forget that the most basic right, other than protection from arbitrary imprisonment, has been and is the right to property. Constitutional courts are empowered to invalidate majority decisions that they see as violating constitutionally protected property rights. They may or may not do it: sometimes they rule that "money is speech" but sometimes that it is not. Nevertheless, the minority needing constitutional protection in economically unequal societies consists of those who are propertied. A telling piece of evidence is that constitutional review was more likely to be introduced in economically more unequal societies (Harvey 2015).

While the rise of constitutional review has been gradual from 1850 to 1950, it has been vertiginous since then. During

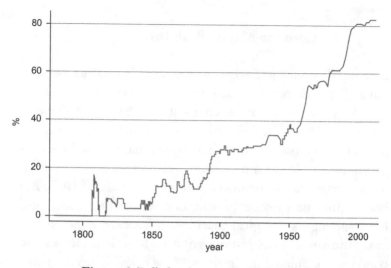

Figure 3.7 *Judicial review in Constitution*

the first few decades of the twenty-first century, more than 80 percent of constitutions provide for judicial review of legislation (based on Ginsburg and Versteeg 2012; Figure 3.7 is reproduced with their permission).

Yet another device protecting some policy realms from temporary majorities is the delegation of authority over them to some non-elected bodies. Most prominently, the argument that re-election-seeking politicians would manipulate the economy to the detriment of economic stability led to the shift of responsibility for monetary policy from elected governments to independent central banks. This shift is more recent and less pronounced but the data also show a secular increase. (Figure 3.8 uses the scale of factual independence created by Cukierman, Edwards, and Tabellini 1992.)

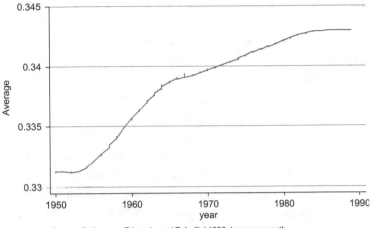

Source: Cukierman, Edwards, and Tabellini 1992. Lowess smooth.

Figure 3.8 *The rise of central bank independence*

Conquests, Reversals, and Substitutions

These then are the historical patterns. They show that while elections spread rapidly, political rights continued for a long time to be restricted to the upper classes and the effects of extending these rights were mitigated by indirect elections and public balloting. These restrictions were abolished over time: franchise became universal, first for men and then for women; elections are now almost everywhere direct and voting is legally secret. Legislatures became more frequently unicameral. Yet the frequency of executive veto power has not diminished, while contra-majoritarian institutions – constitutional review and independent central banks – became more ubiquitous.

With all the caveats about drawing dynamic inferences from these observations, here is a conjecture about the mechanisms that drive this history. Given the extant trenches, those in power make concessions either when they face a foreboding threat from without or when some of them expect to improve their competitive position by finding allies among those currently excluded. These concessions are vulnerable to temporary reversals when outcomes of expanded competition threaten the extant interests. Moreover, whenever particular trenches are conquered, the elites find substitutes to protect their interests. These cycles are repeated over and over.

Have the interests of the propertied become less entrenched as a result of all the trends portrayed above? In several democratic countries economic inequality has returned to levels observed a hundred years ago. The social and economic progress that followed World War II has been arrested if not reversed. Results of elections matter less and less for economic policies. Perhaps Earl Grey was prescient when he announced during an 1831 parliamentary debate on extending suffrage: "The Principal of my Reform is to prevent the necessity of revolution . . . I am reforming to preserve, not to overthrow." The power of elections to transform economic and social relations appears feeble.

4

Jockeying for Partisan Advantage

According to the standard model of political science, what happens in elections is that parties present platforms and candidates, while citizens freely decide which parties to support. Free and politically equal citizens exercise their right to choose governments. Elections express the "Voice of the People."

This portrayal is difficult to square with the fact that in the history of elections defeats of incumbents have been quite rare. The frequency with which incumbents win elections is striking. When they ran, between 1788 and 2008, incumbents won 2,315 of 2,949 elections, 79 percent, with 4:1 odds of winning. Most of the time, in 92 percent of known cases, results of elections were obeyed: someone won, someone lost, and the winner assumed office. In several elections, however, the winner either never made it into office or had

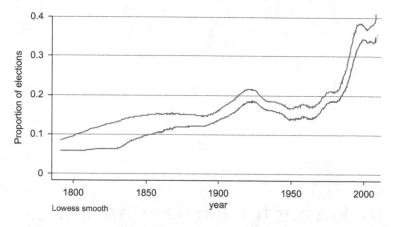

Figure 4.1 *Elections lost by incumbents and elections resulting in partisan alternation over time*

to overcome some usurper first. Hence, partisan alternations in office resulting from elections were even more rare than electoral defeats of incumbents. They occurred in 544 elections out of 2,583 for which this information is available, one in 4.75 elections.

Moreover, as Figure 4.1 shows, elections that resulted in a defeat of the incumbents and in peaceful partisan alternation in office are a very recent phenomenon.

These are not the patterns one would expect to observe according to our standard understanding. The voice heard in many elections does not sound like that of the people but of the rulers or perhaps of those whose interests they protect and promote. Do incumbents really perform so well in office that voters freely want to re-elect them four times out of five? Are voters so risk averse that four times out of five they prefer, as a Mexican proverb has it, a known devil to an angel yet to be revealed? The idea that incumbents' advantage originates from the free choice of voters is just not credible. There is much more to elections than that. What happens on the day of elections is the culmination of a long process of persuasion, but also often of manipulation and repression. What happens during the day of elections may entail intimidation and fraud. And what happens after the elections is not always determined by the announced result: sometimes the incumbent losers do not recognize the defeat; sometimes the defeated opposition storms government palaces.

To understand elections, we need to understand what transpires before, during, and after. Moreover, what happens during elections depends on what would happen after; what transpires before elections depends on what would occur during. Just imagine that the current incumbent fears that if he loses the forthcoming election, he will exit the office through a window. He will do everything he can to avoid this outcome, which may mean not holding elections at all, or holding one without an opposition, or making sure that the opposition has no chance of winning. In contrast, in the banal elections that privilege our lives, the incumbent knows that the eventual defeat means only that she would have to play musical chairs as the leader of the opposition, with a reasonable chance of occupying the chair again, so she may as well abstain from such practices, tolerate a temporary defeat, and wait for the next opportunity to materialize.

While we enter into distinctions and details below, here are just some actions the competing parties may undertake to maximize their chances of winning. They can say "Smith can vote but Gonzales cannot" or "John can but Joan cannot." They can sit across a table and choose their voters – "You get Smith if you give me Gonzales" – which is what the Democratic and Republican incumbents do in the state of New York, with the result that their re-election rate is 99 percent. And then comes the election day in which the number of voters is larger than the number of those eligible to vote, in which some people vote "early and often," and some vote from their grave. Finally, when the results are announced, the incumbent president may say to his defeated opponent, "You poor s.o.b., you may have won the voting but I won the counting," as allegedly did the dictator of Nicaragua, Anastazio Somoza.

Living in solidly democratic countries, we see such practices as aberrant, as anomalies limited to underdeveloped countries or new democracies. But this does not mean that they can be ignored. Repression, intimidation, manipulation of rules, abuse of state apparatus, and fraud are standard instruments of electoral technology. Incumbents do not have complete control over the outcomes of elections but they can and do minimize the probability of being defeated. The mere fact that someone could write a 747-page book just on the history of the ballot shows that minute institutional details matter for the outcomes of elections. And there are innumerable such details regulating electoral competition.

The outcomes of elections may thus sound more like the voice of incumbents than of the people: a standard reference in Spanish-speaking countries was to *gobiernos electores*, governments that elected. Clearly, the availability of these instruments differs across the specific institutional and political contexts. When elections are administered by autonomous and truly independent bodies, when their conduct and their outcomes are subject to validation by truly independent courts, or when the incumbents fear popular reactions to manifest abuses of their power, discretion is limited. But most of the time, incumbents can find ways to influence their chances of winning. Their past performance does matter as do electoral promises, but if incumbents win so often it is because they have access to instruments not available to their challengers. Using these instruments does not relieve the incumbents from the arduous task of electioneering; it only channels their efforts, say, into providing clientelist favors or into outright vote-buying. True, the opposition can also use a variety of tricks to improve its chances. Yet incumbents have an advantage.

Incumbents are able to consolidate their advantage because they constitute a legislative majority and because they direct public bureaucracies. Although at times they are constrained by independent courts, control over legislation grants incumbents an opportunity to adopt legal instruments in their favor. In turn, as principals of ostensibly non-partisan bureaucracies, they can instrumentalize them for partisan purposes. Control over the apparatuses of repression plays a particularly important role in undermining all or some opposition. Exchange of favors for financial resources is yet another source of advantage. And, when all fails, fraud is the last resort. When these instruments can be and are used, even pluralistic elections are not competitive. These points are developed and illustrated by examples below.

Voting and Electing: Opposition

Voting is a physical act: shouting someone's name, raising a hand, placing a particular piece of paper in a box, pulling a lever, or touching a screen. But the political consequences of this act have differed profoundly across countries and epochs. Voting is not the same as electing; indeed, it may have no relation to electing.

The crucial issue in organizing any political order is whether to allow the existence of political opposition(s). According to Hofstadter (1969: 9):

When they [the Founders] began their work, they spoke a great deal – indeed they spoke almost incessantly – about freedom, and they understood that freedom requires some latitude for opposition. But they were far from clear how opposition should make itself felt, for they also valued social unity or harmony, and they had not arrived at the view that opposition, manifested in organized popular parties, could sustain freedom without fatally shattering such harmony.

Such views did not imply that elected positions could not be contested. Yet, even when contested, these election pitched individuals who shared no programs and no labels with candidates in other districts. In modern language, everyone ran as "independents." The right of (some) individuals to compete against the incumbents was not in question. The two issues were whether the people could speak and associate to criticize incumbent governments between elections and whether groups of people could contest elections together, as parties.

Although representative government has meant that rulers have to be authorized by elections, the proper role of the people in between elections was and remains ambiguous. Madison observed that what distinguished the American from the ancient republics "lies in the total exclusion of the people, in their collective capacity from any share in the government" (*Federalist* #63). He seems to have meant it literally, that the people should leave governing to their representatives "as a defense against their own temporary errors and delusions." The last Act of the French Assemblée decreed in 1791 that "No society, club, association of citizens can have, in no form, a political existence, nor exercise any kind of inspection over the act of constituted powers and legal authorities; under no pretext can they appear under a collective name, whether to form petitions or deputations, participate in public ceremonies, or whatever other goal." While not willing to go that far, Joseph Schumpeter (1942: 295) admonished voters that they "must understand that, once they elected an individual, political action is his business not theirs. This means that they must refrain from instructing him what he is to do . . ." And, in 1956, Walter Lippman insisted that the duty of citizens, "is to fill the office and not to direct the office-holder" (p. 73). As Margaret Thatcher would say, "You had your chance, you elected me, now I govern, and you shut up."

While suffrage was the center of political conflicts until roughly the end of World War I, the right to organize between elections and to contest them has become the central issue of politics during the twentieth century. Although uncontested elections were frequent in Latin America during the nineteenth century, with sporadic repression of opposition, this repression was typically short-lived. Some people who came to power by force held elections while banning all opposition, but such elections were normally proclaimed as exceptional, necessitated by particular circumstances. The idea of elections without opposition as a permanent form of political organization was a late innovation. Such elections were first held in Italy in 1934 and in the Soviet Union in 1936. After World War II, Lenin's invention of one-party systems spread to countries under Soviet domination, as well as to many newly independent states in Africa and Asia.

The right to oppose is a conquest. It is feeble and reversible. Moreover, not all who claim the right to oppose for themselves tolerate opposition from others. Consider the history of Russia, where this right was institutionalized as an effect of the revolution of 1905, suppressed by the communists in 1918 after their defeat in the elections to the Constitutional Assembly, restored when communism fell in 1991, and where it is now eroding again.

Hofstadter's (1969: 7) observation that "The normal view of governments about organized opposition is that it is intrinsically subversive and illegitimate" continues to be haunting. The idea that opposition to government policies does not necessarily signify treason or obstruction was first recognized in Great Britain in a parliamentary speech of 1828. But what kind of opposition is loyal and what kind subversive? Must opposition to government policies be channelled through the framework of representative institutions or can people act in any way they please? Ambedkar, the father of the Indian Constitution, thought that while civil disobedience was appropriate under colonial rule, it is "nothing but the Grammar of Anarchy" under democracy. The founders of representative institutions were highly ambivalent about these questions and we are not any clearer about them today. Democracies do grant rights to speak and to associate, but these rights have been tenuous. The limits of rightful opposition are being tested daily, for example, when governments repeatedly declare that "protests are a part of democracy but violence and law-breaking is not" (former British Prime Minister David Cameron on a demonstration by students).

All incumbent rulers want to limit the chances of being deposed. They can attempt to prevent collective opposition from arising, they can make the life of the opposing parties difficult between elections, and they can use incumbency to affect outcomes of elections. But they cannot do it too blatantly. Elections without a choice reduce the claim that the people rules to the unverifiable pretense that the rulers do the best possible on their behalf, the same claim as when rulers are not elected at all. While rulers always claim that they are wanted by the people, only elections that entail the possibility of incumbents being ousted can test this claim, to grant it credibility. Setting the right balance between restricting the opposition and maintaining the belief that people are able to choose is thus a delicate operation.

Instruments at the Disposal of Incumbents

Manipulation of Rules

Elections must inextricably entail some rules that regulate who can vote, whether voting is direct or indirect, secret or public, compulsory or voluntary, how votes are aggregated, and so on. And rules affect outcomes. Even minute details, such as the form or the color of ballots, location of the polling places, or the day of the week when voting takes place, can affect the result. Hence, elections are inextricably manipulated. "Manipulated" because rules are promulgated by incumbent majorities in their own interest, but these rules are legally adopted and some rules must be adopted if elections are to be a determinate procedure.

This is why it is difficult to judge whether an election is "fair," one of the standards used by various international bodies in evaluating elections. Clearly, some actions of incumbents are so transparent that everyone knows that the particular rules have been devised to favor them: electoral districts in the form of salamander have acquired a name in everyday parlance. But are the US elections unfair because they take place on a weekday, as distinct from most countries, where they are held on Sundays? Elections have to take place on some day. Why would it be unfair to hold them on Tuesdays rather than on Sundays? The argument may be that holding elections on a workday makes it more difficult for poorer people to vote and biases the electorate in favor of the party that enjoys support among the wealthier potential voters. But if elections were held on Sundays, wealthy people would rather spend the day in their country houses than vote, so that results would be biased in favor of the other party. I am certain that some normative philosopher could solve this conundrum, but the fact is that rules have consequences, elections must follow some rules, and incumbents have a disproportionate influence over these rules.

Depending on particular constitutional arrangements, rules regulating elections consist of constitutional provisions, ordinary laws, decrees, or administrative orders. These rules are adopted following constitutional provisions (and may be subject to adjudication by courts), they are general, public, and announced *ex ante*, thus constituting legal norms. If the electoral system – the rules transforming votes into parliamentary seats – has changed 11 times in France since 1875, it is because successive majorities constitutionally empowered to do so have passed laws following proper procedures. Note that constitutions, including other fundamental laws, vary in the electoral provisions they leave to the discretion of current majorities: the electoral system is not embedded in French constitutions, as it is in some other countries, but subject to ordinary legislation. In any case, manipulation of rules is a public, overt action. These laws may be "unfair": it is perhaps unfair that someone who received a minority of the popular vote would be declared as the winner. But they are laws.

Because they constitute legal norms, rules must appear as universalistic and fair. If the right to vote is extended to citizens residing abroad, the justification is formulated in terms of rights even when the true reason is that these people are expected to vote for the incumbents. Voter identification cards in the United States are portrayed as a measure to avoid fraud even if they are intended to make voting more difficult for poor people. Before the 2007 Russian parliamentary election, the *Duma* passed 22 laws regulating elections, one of them prohibiting "negative campaigning." Clearly, negative campaigning is not a practice that ennobles the spirit, but what the Putin legislators meant was simply criticism of the government.

Enumerating such rules would be pointless because their

list would be endless. They comprise major laws regulating who can compete and who can vote, apportionment of voters to electoral districts, rules that regulate campaign finance and access to media, and the formulae to transform votes into parliamentary seats. But they also include innumerable minor provisions that may be no less consequential.

In the end, incumbents who have a sufficient majority and are unencumbered by judicial or other forms of independent supervision should be able to win elections relying on manipulation alone. If they do not, it is because they are so unpopular that they would lose under any rules or because they miscalculate.

Partisan Use of the State Apparatus

Domingo Santa Maria, the President of Chile between 1881 and 1886, unabashedly admitted, "Giving away votes to unworthy people, to the irrational passions of the parties, and even with universal suffrage, is a suicide for a ruler and I will not commit suicide before a chimera." This must also have been the view of the French Prime Minister, Jean-Baptiste de Vilèlle, who issued in 1822 a circular instructing "All those who are members of my ministry must, to keep their jobs, contribute within the limits of their right to the election of MPs sincerely attached to the government." Such frankness is exceptional, but the practice of instrumentalizing the state apparatus for electoral purposes has been ubiquitous.

The tension between partisan politics and universalistic administration is built into the structure of state institutions. Elected politicians may have universalistic, partisan, or personal goals. They may want their country to progress; they may want to stay in office, and may have their own ambitions. Universalistic interests are shared across the political spectrum, but partisan interests oppose teams of like-minded politicians seeking to win and retain public office. Personal ambitions lead politicians to compete with their partisan colleagues. They are advanced if politicians loyally serve the party and if the party wins elections: hence, politicians are motivated to prioritize partisan interests.

Elected politicians, however, are not the ones who implement public decisions. In all states, implementation is delegated to specialized organizations, public bureaucracies. The public bureaucracy is supposed to implement decisions made by elected politicians. It is not supposed to be autonomous. Yet it is also supposed to be non-partisan. This situation exposes bureaucracies to conflicting pressures. If a bureaucracy implements decisions of governing politicians, it is an instrument for consolidating partisan advantage. In turn, if bureaucracy is autonomous, then it is not an instrument of the public. Ideally, one would want a bureaucracy that implements those decisions by politicians that are in the general interest of the public without becoming an instrument of those interests that are merely partisan. But this first-best solution is not feasible.

Some years ago, when I was living in Chicago, the tires of my car froze into the ice created by the overnight cold. I called the city government and nothing happened. After a wait of some days – ice never melts in Chicago – my wife, who knew better, called the Democratic precinct captain. He was at our door in a few minutes, pointing out that we had not voted in the last municipal election. We assured him that we were registered Democrats, promised that we would vote in the next election, and an hour later the ice was chipped away by a city crew. Guided by partisan interest, the public bureaucracy was buying our votes by selectively providing public services, while voters in the Republican precincts of the city could only swear at the municipal government, regardless of the urgency of their needs.

The story will be immediately recognized by people in many countries under the names of "clientelism," "nepotism," and the like. Exchange of public resources, whether money, services, or jobs for efforts in favor of the governing party or simply for votes is possible because bureaucrats are agents of partisan politicians. The elected principals can set incentives for the ostensibly non-partisan bureaucrats by conditioning their continued employment, promotions, salaries, or favors to their kin on their partisan loyalty. True, partisan principals face a trade-off between competence of their bureaucratic agents and partisan loyalties. To the extent that probabilities of re-election depend on government performance, elected politicians want their agents to be competent; to the extent that these probabilities depend on partisan efforts, the principals want their agents to be loyal. Nevertheless, whether they are recruited on a meritocratic or purely partisan basis, public officials are subject to pressures from their elected superiors to act in partisan interest. Even when public bureaucracy is protected by statutes, all that members of the bureaucracy can do is go public. But whistle-blowing is not an effective form of oversight.

Some bureaucracies are more important than others. Control over security apparatus, particularly secret services, is crucial. Loyal intelligence agencies are a powerful tool of incumbents. Control over courts is a precious instrument, as in Malaysia where a court obediently sentenced the main political rival of the prime minister for homosexuality. Tax administration can also be a valuable instrument, widely used in Putin's Russia to blackmail or imprison potential opponents. Regulatory agencies can engage in politically targeted enforcement. With these institutions in hand, incumbents can harass the opposition with a full appearance of legality. Partisan control over procurement agencies that purchase goods and services from the private sector opens room for purchasing political support. Control over agencies that collect and publicize economic indices, such as the rate of inflation or of poverty, allows governments to hide negative effects of government policies from the public, albeit not always credibly.

Control over media is also a powerful weapon. Before the advent of radio and television, the standard instrument of control over media was placement of lucrative public announcements in selected newspapers. Public audiovisual media, in turn, are typically regulated by some nominally independent authority charged with the mission of safeguarding their partisan neutrality. Yet the independence of such bodies often turns out to be only nominal, as evidenced by the fact that their composition often changes when new governments arrive in office. Finally, governments can use their regulatory powers to economically undermine private media that oppose them, as did the government of Partido Popular in Spain after 1996, or the government of Christina Kirchner in Argentina in 2011.

In the presence of courts and of public opinion, such practices cannot be as open as they were in the times of Santa Maria or de Vilèlle. But when they are surreptitious, they are hard to detect. The electoral officials in Zanzibar cleverly put beehives in the polling places where voters were known to favor the opposition. When the US Supreme Court decided that college students could vote in places where they study, Republican officials in Ann Arbor located polling places far away from the campus and from public transportation.

Using the state apparatus for partisan purposes is a delicate art, for it must be done without being overdone. For example, Collier and Sater (1996: 58) report that:

Delivering the vote was a vital aspect of the Intendant's work. . . . Yet Intendants could at times go too far. . . . When the young Intendant of Colchagua, Domingo Santa Mara [quoted above already as the president], interpreted the president's instructions to win the elections "at all costs" a trifle too enthusiastically, this was seized by his enemies as the pretext for his dismissal.

In Spain in 1872 votes for the opposition were inflated by the government, to "illuminate electoral freedom" (*"para que realizaran la luminosa libertad electoral"*). When in 1960 South Korean election officials reported the vote for President Sigman Rhee's hand-picked successor to be 100 percent, they were instructed to scale it down to 75 percent.

Repression

The use or the threat of physical force to repress opposition has been widespread, but its range differs greatly. In some instances repression is used to prevent collective organization of any opposition, in some to squash the opposition that is already organized, in some to prevent electoral participation of specific political forces, and in some just to eliminate from the public sphere particular ideas or particular opponents.

Repression designed to prevent the emergence of any collective opposition is a permanent operation, not limited to elections. When it functions well, intimidation is sufficient, so that the use of force does not need to be intensified before elections. Consolidated one-party systems tend to be peaceful, even if they are vulnerable to periodic eruptions of mass protest. Elections in which 99 percent of eligible voters turned out at the polls and the ruling party received 99 percent of the vote were a routine ceremony in the communist systems.

Once some kind of opposition becomes public, however, repressing it requires brute force: opposition leaders are murdered, jailed, or sent into exile. Recent political science studies focus almost exclusively on situations in which a government interacts with an already constituted opposition group or reacts to a public protest. Such situations, however, occur only if repression has not been effective to begin with, so that they represent failures of repressive regimes. In the history of Latin America, elections in which incumbents abused their power often provoked armed rebellions under the name of "revolutions." In recent years, electoral protests have assumed the guise of "color revolutions": peaceful popular protests against results of elections deemed to have been unfair. The ability of the police is often insufficient to handle such situations: when the opposition constitutes a mass movement, the armed forces are often called to intervene.

Repressing all opposition is not always necessary to stay in power. Many incumbent rulers are more selective, preventing competition from only some ideologies, parties, or individuals, while selecting the political forces that are permitted to organize and compete. In the Ivory Coast, Kenya, and Zambia, nationality requirements were introduced ad hoc to prevent candidacies of the most popular opponents. In several instances, members of previous governments were banned from politics. In Iran, all candidates have to be approved by a religious authority. Token opposition yields some credibility to incumbents' victories so it is often tolerated and sometimes even encouraged. The Brazilian military created an official opposition party (only to discover that this party won the election and actually opposed them). While making life difficult for other opponents, President Putin encouraged the entry into the *Duma* of communists, who made sufficient noise to generate the appearance of opposition but did not threaten his power. Even regimes generally considered as democracies sometimes ban forces dubbed as anti-democratic.

Such uses of repression are overt and often brutal. Some forms are more subtle. During the tenure of Mayor Richard

Daley, the Chicago City Council adopted a building code that was deliberately impossible to comply with, thus providing the Democratic machine with an instrument to selectively harass the opponents. The French President Nicolas Sarkozy received every morning a report from the Chief of Police about the private life of his potential rivals, with details such as the cost of dresses purchased the previous day by the Socialist politician, Ségolène Royal. President Richard Nixon used the Internal Revenue Service as well as the Bureau of Narcotics to harass opponents of the Vietnam War. I suspect that such petty repression is endemic but it is also covert, so evidence is hard to come by.

Election Financing

Politics costs money: this much is inescapable. Parties need money to exist, to organize election campaigns, to survey public opinion, to bring their supporters to the polls, to persuade those undecided to vote for them. They need to cover costs of meeting rooms, transportation, printing their materials, and access to television. So it is only natural that they try to find money wherever they can.

They can find money only where the money is. Some of it is in state coffers but much in private purses. The influx of money to politics should not be reduced to "corruption." True, corruption scandals abound: suitcases filled in cash are found in the prime minister's office, political parties are found to have bank accounts in Switzerland, local governments operate systematic bribe schedules on their contractors – the list goes on and on. Moreover, such scandals are by no means limited to less developed countries or to young democracies: these examples are drawn from Germany, Spain, France, Italy, and Belgium. But reducing the political role of money to "corruption" is deeply misleading. Conceptualized as "corruption," the influence of money becomes something anomalous, out of the ordinary. We are told that when special interests bribe legislators or bureaucrats, politics is corrupt. And then nothing needs to be said when special interests make legal political contributions. When the government steals money from the public sector, as did the Brazilian Workers' Party (PT) from the state oil company, Petrobras, we think of it as corruption. But when parties are financed by private firms, as are the Brazilian opposition parties, we do not see it as such. In order to exist and to participate in elections, political parties need money; because election results matter for the private interests, they understandably seek to befriend parties and influence the results of elections: the logic of political competition is inexorable. That the same acts are legal in some countries and illegal in other systems – US political financing practices would constitute corruption in most democracies – is in the end of secondary importance. The infiltration of money into politics is a structural feature of elections.

The information about political financing is scant. To some extent this lack of knowledge is due to the very nature of the phenomenon: legally or not, money infiltrates itself into politics in ways that are intended to be opaque. A general conclusion of surveys conducted in 22 countries by the National Democratic Institute for International Affairs is that "Little is known about the details of money in political parties or in campaigns. Political party financing patterns are extremely opaque . . ." The main fact that emerges from studies of campaign financing is that those who receive and spend more money win. This much has been observed at least in the United States, Brazil, Chile, France, Japan, South Korea, and Uruguay. And incumbents get more private money than challengers. One should not, however, jump to the conclusion that incumbents win because they spend more money. The question is whether money buys votes or votes generate money. Moreover, if it does, how does money buy votes? Is it because political advertising changes voters' preferences, because some voters are "impressionable," or is it because campaign contributions finance the activities of parties – ranging from registration efforts to provision of transportation – to bring their supporters to the polls; hence, they differentially affect turnout? Whose votes does money buy: those of the undecided or of people who otherwise would not vote? To date, no consensus has been reached regarding the effectiveness of campaign spending on vote shares.

To appreciate how complex these causal mechanisms can be, consider the study of Grossman and Helpman (2001), attempting to distinguish the role of money in buying both party platforms and votes in the US context. In their story parties maximize the probability of winning a majority of seats, while special interest groups maximize the welfare of their members. Voters come in two kinds: strategic voters consider their interests, while impressionable voters are influenced by campaign advertising. Special interests make campaign contributions, politicians choose policies, and voters vote; not necessarily in this order because contributions can play a twofold role. They can be used early in the campaign to induce parties to announce platforms that are to the liking of the lobbies or they can be used once the platforms have been announced to sway voters to vote for the party closer to the lobby. Their conclusions are that:

1 To influence their platforms, special interests contribute to both parties, giving more to the party that is the *ex ante* favorite to win.

2 If the resulting platforms are the same, special interests are indifferent as to which party would win and contribute no more.

3 If the resulting platforms differ, special interests contribute additional funds to tilt the election in favor of the party closers to their interests.

"Overall," Grossman and Helpman conclude (2001: 339), "the contributions bias the policy outcome away from the public interest both by influencing the parties' positions and perhaps by tilting the election odds."

In the end, however, these analytical complexities do not alter the basic fact: whether private interests want governments they like to be elected or to secure favors with the future governments even if they are not to their liking, private money flows into the coffers of parties or politicians. Even if the impact of campaign expenditures on votes is lower for the incumbents, who already enjoy a high level of support, than for the challengers, incumbents get more of it either because they are more likely to win or because they are already in the pocket of private interests which want them to stay in office. Regulation of political financing does matter: removal of state limits on campaign spending in the United States led to increased Republican vote shares and the election of more conservative candidates (Harvey 2016). There are important cross-country differences in allowing private contributions, as well as in transparency requirements, and they seem to be consequential (Prat 1999). But money is probably never absent from elections, as it has so many opaque ways to infiltrate itself into politics – a threat to finance the entry of an opponent may be sufficient to influence the incumbent even when no money is actually spent.

Fraud

Fraud is a failure. It is the last resort, used when all else fails. Fraud is not the same as manipulation. Manipulation consists of setting rules that affect the probability that the incumbent would be re-elected; fraud is a violation of the extant formal rules, however biased these may be. Breaking into the office of the opposition party to steal its secrets, as in Watergate, is fraud because it violates a general prohibition against burglary. Buying votes constitutes fraud when it is prohibited by specific rules. So is casting votes of people whose spirits have passed to a better world. The technology of fraud is highly varied but, in almost all of its forms, fraudulent activity is clandestine. Incumbents may make unfair rules, but they do not want to be seen violating them.

True, the line between fraud and manipulation is slippery. Buying individual votes for cash is fraud but pumping up the economy on the eve of an election need not be. In the Mexican presidential election of 2006, the defeated candidate vociferously claimed that he was defrauded. Most of his complaints had no base, but one shows how slippery the line sometimes is: according to the Mexican Constitution, the incumbent president is prohibited from campaigning for his successor and President Fox repeatedly violated this prohibition.

Fraud is not a simple operation, because it has to be prepared in advance. As Posada-Carbó (2000: 634) emphasizes:

Electoral fraud involved a long procedure, open to subtle and not so subtle machinations, which started with the formation of the electoral register and followed a set of identifiable steps, including "tricks" to register the largest number of voters, to influence the composition of electoral boards and the selection of juries at the polling station, to mobilize the largest number of voters on the polling days, to invalidate when convenient certain electoral tables, and of course to stuff the ballot box.

Because self-interested speech – speech that can be predicted from interests – is not credible, claims of fraud made by defeated opponents must be taken with a grain of salt. As a result, our attention is attracted only to flagrant instances. But there appear to be many. The subtitle of a history of fraud in the United States is "A Political Tradition." In Costa Rica, parties used 47 different types of fraud, including the inappropriate exclusion of voters, the purchase of votes, changes in the location of polling places on election day, and alterations of ballots. In early twentieth-century France, voters were given half a banknote prior to election and the other half if the candidate won; in Chicago, they were given one shoe before and the second one after: the origins of the expression "when the other shoe drops."

Fraud is not a phenomenon of the distant past. In Palermo, in the 1970s, Italian Christian Democrats distributed public-sector jobs along with free pasta and shoes in exchange for support. In 1993, in Taiwan, the Kuomintang bought 14,090 votes for 300 Taiwanese dollars each. In the Philippines, in 2001, 10.1 percent of voters reported having been offered gifts; in Argentina, in 2001, 12 percent were offered financial incentives; and in Mexico, in 2000, as many as 26.1 percent were. In 2004, in eastern Kentucky, a candidate for district judgeship was accused by prosecutors of giving $50 checks to voters. Still, fraud is rare in most countries, the United States included, and it is even less frequently decisive.

It does matter how elections are administered. Consider four common arrangements:

1 The executive administers elections and the legislature certifies the results.
2 The executive administers and a judicial organ, perhaps specialized, certifies.
3 An independent body administers and a judicial organ certifies.
4 An independent body administers and certifies.

When representative institutions were established, the first system was instituted everywhere. Administration of elections by a body that was independent of the executive was an innovation introduced in Canada in 1920, followed by Chile in 1925 and Uruguay in 1932. As of 2006, the first system still prevailed in 26 percent of countries covered, in 15 percent elections were administered by the executive and an independent judicial body certified, while electoral management bodies were nominally independent in 55 percent of countries (in the remaining 4 percent, elections were not held). Obviously, as studies of independent central banks have demonstrated, nominal independence does not guarantee an effective one and, as the US 2000 election demonstrated, even judicial bodies can have partisan preferences. But it is clear that the first system allows the incumbent wide latitude: fraudulently elected supporters of the incumbent have no incentives to question results of the election. In turn, the independence of the Mexican Instituto Federal Electoral, established in reaction to the electoral fraud of 1988, was crucial in allowing the victory of the opposition in 2000. Independent observers can also reduce fraud, if they have strong capabilities to detect irregularities and are able to make credible statements regarding the degree of fraud.

Competitive and Non-Competitive Elections

Elections are competitive when voters can determine who wins them, most importantly when they can dismiss the incumbents if they so wish. Competitive elections are not "fair": elections have to be conducted by some rules and all rules bias the chances one way or another. They are never completely "clean": there is no way to prevent the competing parties from using some trick to enhance their chances.

One estimate is that between 19 and 36 percent of presidential elections around the world were "flawed," "corrupt," or "fraudulent" during the 1975–2000 period. Incumbents have an advantage because they can manipulate rules, instrumentalize the state apparatus, exploit financial opportunities, and if all else fails tinker with the results. Hence, if we think that elections are competitive when incumbents are about as likely to lose as to win, we should be prepared to see that such elections are rare. Yet, even if the chances are unequal, as long as results of elections are uncertain, as long as the competing parties can influence only the probability of their victory but must leave room for surprise, elections are competitive.

5

Conclusion
What is Inherent in Elections?

The examples cited above ranged from Argentina to Zimbabwe and spanned the past 200 years because elections are not all the same. Several aspects of elections – qualifications to be eligible for office and to vote, secrecy of the ballot, the institutions that mediate the relation between votes and legislative seats – evolved over time in the direction of making political participation more extensive and more free. Elections without any opposition are pretty much a phenomenon of the past. Yet perhaps – at least this is what many observers think – many political leaders have learned to control the results of elections while preserving the appearance of competition: this is the "new," "competitive," or "soft" authoritarianism. Hence, various aspects of elections continue to differ from country to country.

The question to be asked is whether, with all these variations, there is something that is inherent in elections, some features that all elections share. We already know that not all events that are called "elections" in fact serve to select rulers. But have elections which the incumbent rulers are certain to win something in common with competitive ones? Is protection of property from majority rule inevitable? Can elections be free from the maneuvers of competing parties to influence their results independently of what people want? Answers to such questions are to some extent inevitably arbitrary because even if all elections share some features, these features come in gradations, so that such answers are in the eye of the beholder. But here are the candidates for such universal features.

All elections, including those in which no one is selected, make rulers nervous. Consider the extreme case: elections without opposition. Many dictators, communist ones prominently, every few years proudly reported that they won 99.1 percent of the popular vote. No one believes that such elections indicate anything about the true preferences of the citizens: not those who had voted, not those for whom they had voted, and not external observers. The purpose of such elections is different, namely to intimidate any potential opposition. Being able to get millions of people to appear in designated places at designated times and to manifest their compliance with the regime is not an easy undertaking. Hence, such elections show that the dictatorship can make the dog perform tricks, that it can intimidate 99 percent of the population, so that any opposition is futile. Other authoritarian regimes do want to pass as democracies, so they allow some opposition, hold their vote down, and claim it to be the free will of the people. Yet they still worry about numbers. For example, while under communism the target for turnout was 99 percent, the ruling Partido Revolucionario Institucional (PRI) in Mexico did not want the turnout to fall below 65 percent. Once such targets become known – and they become known from the result of past elections – failing to reach them, any decline of numbers, indicates a weakening of political control and opens doors to oppositional activities. Indeed, the fall of communism in Poland was forecast by the results of the local elections in 1984, when turnout failed to reach 75 percent: everyone knew that the regime could not control the situation any longer. Even rulers who hold non-competitive elections must be concerned about their results. Elections make rulers nervous even when their tenure is not directly at stake because failure to produce the expected targets makes them vulnerable to removal by other mechanisms, whether military intervention or popular mobilization. Relying on repression alone makes them hostage to the coercive apparatuses, which should make them even more nervous than elections. Thus, making rulers nervous is not limited specifically to competitive elections. Indeed, there is evidence that authoritarian regimes exhibit electoral business cycles, that is, they increase consumption before elections. Even when rulers run sham elections, they have to pay at least some attention to what voters want.

It is unreasonable to expect that competing parties might abstain from doing whatever they can to enhance their electoral advantage. Even when their actions are tightly regulated and extensively monitored, there are always ways to influence the results. For one, the current majority has legal ways to change some rules to their advantage: just think of voter registration laws or apportionment. The courts or some other independent bodies may invalidate some such attempts but not always have sufficient reason or the will to do so: for example, there are many ways to divide districts, each with electoral consequences, which are not blatantly discriminatory. Should the value of the work of volunteers be counted as a campaign expenditure? The French courts decided in one instance that they should be and invalidated a mayoral election for exceeding expenditure limits, but other courts may not. Should mail or early voting be permitted? Should residents of a country

residing abroad have the right to vote? All these decisions
bias the expected results in someone's favor, but there may be
no constitutional reasons to invalidate them. What about the
selective use of building code violations under Mayor Daley in
Chicago? After all, the city bureaucracy cannot inspect everyone. What about the police reports to President Sarkozy?
Neither of these practices were ever found to be illegal. There
are always ways, and if such ways increase the probability of
winning, office-seeking politicians will use them.

It is also unreasonable to expect elected governments,
whatever majority elected them, not to pay special attention to those who control productive resources. Capitalism
is a system in which most productive resources are owned
privately, which means that the crucial decisions affecting
everyone, those concerning investment and employment, are
made by private actors seeking to maximize profit. Because
everyone depends on these decisions, all governments have
to anticipate the effect of their policies on the decisions of
firms. This much is thus structural: an effect of the property
structure of a capitalist society. Private ownership of productive resources limits the range of outcomes that can ensue
from the democratic process. Governments, regardless of
who occupies their heights, who elected them and with what
intentions, are constrained in any capitalist economy by the
fact that crucial economic decisions, those affecting employment and investment, are a private prerogative. Moreover,
even within these structural limits, people with larger economic resources can use them to influence the outcomes of
elections and the policies of the elected governments.

All these features do come in gradations. But suppose that
political rights are universal and that the capacity of incumbent rulers to control the results of elections is limited, so
that elections are truly competitive. What could we expect of
such elections?

Part II

WHAT ELECTIONS CAN AND CANNOT ACHIEVE

6

Introduction to Part II

What should we expect of competitive elections?

Elections are not pretty. While politicians have to pretend to be inspirational, claiming that their lofty ideals will lead us to a radiant future, they use every hook or crook to win. They posture, monger, and deceive. They make promises they know to be infeasible, spend much of their energies smearing each other, tinker with rules when they can and evade them when they cannot, and try to mute the voice of the people who may be opposed to them. No wonder that quite a few people either just turn off or dream of somehow eliminating the features of elections that offend while preserving the very mechanism of selecting rulers.

Not all the reasons for which people complain about elections are good reasons: some are based on a misunderstanding of elections as a mechanism by which we make collective decisions. Contrary to persistent complaints that elections do not offer choice, even if at the time we go to the polls all we can choose is "tweedledum and tweedledee," "Pepsi or

Coke," "Gin and Tonic or Tonic and Gin," as various pundits have it, it does not mean that as a society we have not made a choice. Consider an extreme situation, in which different parties propose exactly the same set of policies. They offer them because they believe these policies are what a majority of us want. True, politicians try to persuade and seduce, but they look at the surveys and the encounter groups, they lick their fingers to gauge the winds of public opinion, and then try to guess what we want. Parties promise what they think would make them most likely to win. Had a majority wanted something different, competing parties would have offered something different. Hence, the electorate, as a collectivity, chooses even when none of us has a choice at the polling place.

Voting is not an action that makes individuals feel empowered, but this is not a valid reason for complaint. In a large electorate, no one can say "I voted for A, so A won." In fact, we cast our votes and then rush home and turn on the TV to learn, often uncertain late into the night, who won. From the individual point of view, results of an election are like those of flipping a coin: there is no causal relation between action and outcome. The value of elections is not that each voter has real influence on the final result, but that collective choice is made by summing the total of individual wills. Even if individuals see their own vote as ineffective, they should value voting as a procedure for making collective choices, and there is dramatic evidence that often they do: some people have sacrificed their lives for the ideal of free elections. To value elections, it is sufficient that "Both governors and governed must recognize 'will-revealing' procedures and view them as communicating instructions, which governing agencies are then expected to execute as a matter of course" (Bird 2000: 567).

We value elections because they are the second best to what we would really like: each of us being free to do whatever one wants. We have to live together and to live together we must be governed. No one likes to be ordered to do what one does not want to do or to be forbidden to do what one wants to, but governed we must be. And because we cannot all govern at the same time, at best we can choose by whom and how we would be governed, reserving the right to get rid of governments we do not like. This is what elections enable us to do.

Are there good reasons to think that if rulers are selected through contested elections their decisions will be rational, that governments will be representative, the economy will perform well, the distribution of income will be egalitarian, and people will live in liberty and peace? These are the questions analyzed below. Note that the consequences I discuss are not the only outcomes of conceivable interest; for example, I do not enter into complex issues of justice. I leave the list open as an invitation to the reader.

It may be that answers to such questions are conditional on some institutional features distinguished above, such as presidentialism and parliamentarism or electoral systems. Yet, while I assume throughout that all of Dahl's (1971) conditions defining elections as contested hold, my purpose is to examine the consequences of the mere fact that governments are freely elected, whatever the methods of election, other institutional features, cultural traditions, or social conditions.

My method in studying these questions is eclectic and opportunistic. Whenever the structure of a problem is sufficiently clear, I rely on deductive arguments. Whenever systematic empirical evidence exists, I bring to bear the "facts." But I also do not shy from trusting authorities, looking for intuitions in particular historical events, or simply asserting prior beliefs.

7

Rationality

Can we expect that if governments are chosen through elections their decisions will be in some sense rational?

The answer depends on what we consider to be "rational." Since the eighteenth century, our political language has been full of concepts that assume there is some state of the world which is best for the entire society, with phrases such as "general will," "common good," "public interest," or "reason of state." National security, prevention of contagious diseases, clean air, or low inflation are examples of candidates for such states of the world. A decision of the government is then rational if it picks the best means to bring this state of the world about. Rationality is much harder to define, however, with regard to issues about which a society is divided. What may be good for some is then bad for others, so that nothing is rational for all.

Is it sufficient that a majority of voters think something is best for all? Or can our common good be identified independently of what any majority happens to think? If the choice of a majority does not identify the public interest, then who or what does? One would think that preventing contagious diseases is in our common interest, but what if a majority votes for a party that opposes compulsory vaccinations? One may believe that breathing clean air is good for all and each of us, but what if a majority votes against pollution controls? What is then rational? Clearly, we have two choices: either we are willing to accept some idea of rationality (and the same holds for justice) that does not depend on the will of a majority or we have to accept that whatever a majority wants is rational. Neither solution makes us easy. As Lagerspetz (2010: 30) observed, "there is something deeply disturbing in the idea that a purely mechanical, content-free procedure could determine what we should do." Purely procedural rules need not generate wise or virtuous outcomes. Yet the claim that someone knows better regardless of what any number of people may think is an authoritarian claim.

We have reasons to vote in a particular way and these reasons are based on our beliefs about the candidates and their announced goals or about the effects of the policies they propose. Yet elections are a mechanism that aggregates only discrete decisions – we vote for this party or candidate and not for other parties or candidates – not the reasons behind them. Public discussion of issues, "deliberation," may lead to decisions that are reasoned: it may enlighten the reasons for a decision being taken and elucidate the reasons it should not be taken. Even more, these reasons may guide the implementation of the decision, the actions of the government. But the authorization for these actions, including coercion, originates from voting, from counting heads, not from discussion.

The reasons we vote one way or another are shaped during

a long process of persuasion and deliberation, of which voting is only the final act. Hence, it is only natural to wonder whether it makes a difference that people deliberate before voting. In a widespread view, if the process of deliberation satisfies certain criteria – treating everyone as equal, respecting other people's preferences, being open to arguments – then it generates good reasons. Yet these conditions are too demanding to serve as a description of real political debates. In a democracy, we want to persuade others because we know that they will vote on a decision that will bind us, and that means that political communication is inevitably strategic, motivated by the desire for our arguments to prevail. Hillary Clinton should not have been surprised when she declared, "I did not realize how sophisticated they [the opponents] would be in conveying messages that were effective politically even though substantively wrong" (interview in *The New York Times*, October 3, 1994). When people do not know some relevant facts, when they are not clear about the effect of policies being proposed, they can be persuaded by "substantively wrong" arguments. Even more, people may listen to arguments and yet vote in favor of what they see as their interests. Whether the reasons behind voting decisions are good or bad ones – the sociology and the psychology of the processes by which people arrive at decisions whether and how to vote is far from clear – the fundamental principle of liberalism is that everyone must be treated as the best judge of their own interests. This is why elections are decided by votes, not by reasons.

Common Interests

The claim that the rulers can act in the best interest of everyone entails the belief that there is something generally shared that can be advanced and promoted: *res publica*, "common good," "general or public interest," "social welfare." This belief is canonical, even if it comes in variants. The point of departure is either that the society is naturally harmonious – the people is united as one body – or at least that the goal of politics should be to maintain harmony and cooperation. The political myth put forward by all rulers, regardless of who they are, how they come to power, and how they rule, is that "the people" is united, that there are no fundamental divisions in society, that interests and values are harmonious, and that political life can be guided by consensus. "United we stand" is a slogan used by all rulers to induce compliance with whatever they stand for themselves. As a Polish Minister of Defense, Antoni Macierewicz, recently declared, "You have only one Party. This Party is Poland" (TVN, November 19, 2016). In turn, irreconcilable conflicts can be eliminated by excluding "the enemies of the nation" – "foreign elements," "class enemies," "traitors" – from the body of "the people."

The myth of unity is incessantly propagated by appeals to nationalism, evocations of common roots even in the face of divergent origins, celebrations of national holidays, anthems, and flags, expressions of pride in the national army or in the national performance in the Olympics, . . . the list goes on. Even in countries that hold partisan elections, governments cannot admit that they act in partisan interests: electoral victories are always followed by a "unity" speech. Salvador Allende's declaration, "*No soy Presidente de todos los Chilenos*" ("I am not the President of all the Chileans") was an enormous blunder.

"Unity," "harmony," "consensus," and "cooperation" are normatively attractive. They offer the prospect of rationality, justice, and freedom: they make a world that is more rational and more just than conflicts processed through purely procedural rules. If interests and values are harmonious, everyone wants to live under the same laws. "Consensus" means that everyone wants the same outcome to prevail, so that it makes no difference who makes collective decisions and by what procedures. Anyone can decide for all. Moreover, collective decisions are self-implementing: if someone else tells me to do what I want to do anyway, I do not need to be coerced to obey the decision. As long as interests are harmonious, the rulers derive their authority from pursuing the true common good.

Suppose, then, that there exists some state of the world which is best for each and all; hence, one "correct" decision. Note that if there exists one correct decision, the collective decision-making process is purely "epistemic," just a search for the truth. If either stimulating demand at the cost of fiscal deficit or maintaining fiscal discipline is best for all, the only question facing the community is which is better. Does the electoral process indicate which it is?

An eighteenth-century French genius, Marquis de Condorcet, offered an argument that implies that the majority rule does generate such correct decisions. If each individual is endowed with reason, at least to the extent that each person is more likely to vote for the correct decision than not, then an assembly is more likely to make the right decision than each individual separately. Indeed, as the size of the assembly increases, it becomes almost certain that the assembly will make the correct choice. Majority rule in a large assembly makes it almost infallible. The intuition underlying this argument relies on a stylized situation of a jury facing a decision to convict or acquit someone charged with a crime. Presumably there is some true underlying state of affairs (guilty or not guilty) and members of the jury have no interests other than to administer justice. The same argument can be extended to other realms. Suppose that everyone in a Florida coastal town would be better off if the town were evacuated when a hurricane strikes but not if it does not strike. Each person is more likely to guess rightly whether it will strike than to err, and all vote whether or not to evacuate. Then, again, majority vote is likely to identify correctly what is best for all to do. Moreover, it has been shown that under some conditions collective competence increases with the size of the assembly, even if increasing the size lowers the average individual competence. Hence, collective decision-making by voting is likely to yield decisions superior to those made by any single individual, even an exceptionally wise dictator or a small group.

Yet the argument that majority rule identifies the right answer makes no sense when interest, values, or norms are in conflict. The difference between the jury and the electorate is that while the jury is faced with an issue which has one answer which is correct for each and all individuals, different decisions may be correct for different voters. If I support the right to choose and others the right to life, what is "the" correct decision? The preference of a majority is then no longer a reading of what everyone has in common but simply an expression of what a majority wants. Suppose citizens vote on one issue, taxes. Then some people inevitably gain and some lose from any course of action a government chooses. This difference led Black (1958: 163) to conclude that the Condorcet's argument was irrelevant for the theory of elections:

Now whether there is much or little to be said in favor of a theory of juries arrived at in this way, there seems to be nothing in favor of a theory of elections that adopts this approach. When a judge, say, declares an accused person to be either guilty or innocent, it would be possible to conceive of a test which, in principle at least, would be capable of telling us whether his judgment had been right or wrong. But in the case of elections, no such test in conceivable; and the phrase "the probability of correctness of a voter's opinion" seems to be without definite meaning.

Thus, while the conclusion must be that making decisions by voting is not generally expected to be rational, this is not a deficiency of elections but of the underlying structure of interests. When individual interests are harmonious to the point that individual decisions generate no externalities or when they are compatible to the point that there exists one collective interest that everyone wants to be coercively enforced, voting generates rational decisions and does it better than alternative systems. But when interests or values are in conflict, this concept of rationality does not provide a coherent way to characterize government decisions: the most we can say is that the government does or does not do what a majority wants.

Divergent Interests

There is, however, another way to think about rationality, applicable to situations in which different people want different states of the world to prevail. To introduce it, think first of single issues, such as the rate of taxation or the regulation of abortion. Say a third of the electorate wants the tax rate to be 10 percent, a third wants it to be 30 percent, and a third wants 70 percent, and suppose that individual unhappiness with any policy increases (linearly) as the distance between the policy and their preference increases. We can then ask what policy would minimize collective dissatisfaction, with an answer of 37 percent. Or say that a fifth of citizens want abortion to be banned under all circumstances (0 months), half want it to be allowed up to 3 months, and three tenths want it to be allowed until 6 months. Then the law that bans abortion after 3.3 months will minimize the dissatisfaction of citizens with the the law under which they live. The Austrian legal theorist Hans Kelsen, who first thought in these terms in 1929, called this criterion "autonomy," while the US political scientist who provided a logical proof of this argument, Douglas Rae (1969), called it "political individualism." But whatever we call it, decisions that satisfy this criterion are rational in the sense that they maximize collective welfare given the distribution of individual preferences.

Hence, simple majority rule turns out to be very powerful. If some assumptions hold, most importantly that every vote has equal weight, then simple majority rule, 50 percent plus one, is the unique rule that renders collective decisions rational in the above sense, that is, it minimizes collective dissatisfaction or, when there are only two alternatives, the number of people who live under laws not to their liking. Simple-majority rule optimizes the correspondence between individual preferences and collective policies. Moreover, simple-majority rule is responsive to the contingency that individuals change preferences: the status quo can be altered if enough individuals change their mind.

True, the mere possibility of changing laws does not guarantee that all people would live under laws they like in turn. Some people may have to wait indefinitely. In an electorate in which grandchildren inherit the preferences of their forefathers, a perfectly representative party would remain in office for ever. This possibility haunts democracy in ethnically divided societies. For alternation to be possible, that is, for the chances of victory of particular alternatives to be uncertain, either individual preferences must be changing or the incumbents must err in representing them. And even then people who are unlucky enough to have unpopular preferences will never see them implemented. Yet simple-majority rule maximizes the probability that laws would change when people change preferences.

The Kelsen-Rae argument applies, however, only when people vote on one issue. In fact, when we elect governments we choose a bunch of policies. One party may be for free trade, little redistribution of income, and for limitations on abortion; another may be protectionist, concerned with inequality, and in favor of the right to choose. Under such conditions there are many possible majorities: one may consist of people who support free trade but are liberal on cultural issues; another of people who want to redistribute incomes but favor free trade, and so on. It is then no longer possible to identify one proposal that would beat every other proposal by majority vote (this is what the famous "impossibility theorem" of Kenneth Arrow (1951) demonstrates). Yet elections still bring policy closer to popular preferences than a dictator might. Think graphically of an egg: the yolk consists of all policy combinations that are supported by some majority, while the white includes combinations that would be defeated by every majority in the yolk. A dictator can choose policies in the entire egg but elections must select one in the yolk. A dictator may choose a bunch of policies that no majority supports, while any outcome of elections must be supported by some majority.

In elections, parties and candidates compete by proposing to pursue different sets of policies. Hence, elections offer us the opportunity to choose among different ways we would be governed, at least among different sets of instructions for the government. The very fact that no one is ever elected unanimously in reasonably clean elections is prima facie evidence that there are people other than those elected who also are seen as having the authority to govern; moreover, that authority is contested. Perhaps the people is not united but divided; perhaps they are united but still disagree on what is better for all: whether elections aggregate interests or judgements, the pluralism of authority is anti-authoritarian. Elections do not generate epistemic or moral authority of those who are elected; they ratify it. We elect those who we believe have authority. Hence, we obey elected leaders not only because elections generate legal authority to command and empower the elected rulers to use legally qualified coercion, but also because at least some of us believe that they were elected because they have the wisdom and the virtue to govern. Moreover, it may be true that having seen that a majority recognizes someone as the authority we update our beliefs on the basis of their information, so that elections do enhance the belief that those elected have authority. The distinctive feature of "authoritarianism" is not the use of coercion to evoke compliance. True, under democracy, coercion must be legally qualified and its use is protected by institutionalized safeguards. Yet the rate of incarceration in the oldest democracy in the world is the highest in the world. All political systems coerce: we could not live together without being coerced. The distinction lies in the use of force to prevent potentially competing authorities from being heard, not the absence of reason but its monopoly, which under authoritarianism must be protected by repression and censorship.

Conclusion

Elections generate instructions for governments to pursue policies that reflect a distribution of popular preferences. If these preferences differ, whatever the reasons behind them, the instructions given to the government are those of a majority of voters. And, as Simmel (1950 [1908]: 241) observed, "a mere majority decision probably does not yet contain the full truth because, if it did, it ought to have succeeded in uniting *all* votes." Disagreements indicate that truth is not manifest, that any decision may be erroneous. A "hung jury," a body that cannot reach unanimity even after all the deliberation, does not provide certain guidance as to how each and all of us ought to act. If some want us to do one thing and others another, what ought we do in common? The only way we can single out particular decisions as "rational" in a society with heterogeneous preferences is that they minimize the popular dissatisfaction with the outcome. Simple-majority rule does identify such decisions. These decisions are not unique when we make several decisions at the same time but at least any decision generated by majority rule enjoys the support of some majority, which need not be true when decisions are reached by methods other than voting. So in this sense elections do generate rationality. The question, then, becomes whether governments which are elected, and which have to expect that they will face the test of elections in the future, have reasons to obey voters' instructions.

8

Representation, Accountability, and Control over Governments

Can we expect that if governments are elected they will do what a majority of citizens wants them to do and not do what a majority does not want them to do? Are elections an effective instrument of control over governments?

Governments are representative if they do what is best for the people, act in the best interests of at least a majority of citizens. There are four possible reasons why governments would represent interests of the people:

1 Because only those persons who are public-spirited offer themselves for public service and they remain uncorrupted by power while in office.
2 Because, while individuals who offer themselves for public service differ in their motivations and in their competence – some candidates for office are selfless and competent

and others are rascals or potential rascals – citizens use their vote effectively to select good candidates, who remain dedicated to the public service while holding office.

3 Because, while anyone who holds office may want to pursue some interests or values different from and costly to the people, citizens use their vote effectively to threaten those who would stray too far from the path of virtue with being thrown out of office and not being able to enjoy its fruits any longer.

4 Because separate powers of government check and balance each other in such a way that, together, they end up acting in people's best interest.

The first possibility should not be dismissed. Many persons who seek public office want to serve the public and some remain dedicated to the public service while in power. If I do not consider this possibility, it is because this way of securing representation is not distinctive of elections. Dictators can be also representative: if they know and if they want to do what people want, nothing prevents them from doing it. The connection between elections and representation cannot depend on luck, on who happens to be the ruler.

A central claim of democratic theory is that elections are a mechanism that systematically causes governments to be representative. This claim is widespread: "representation," or its cognates, is frequently treated as quintessential, if not definitional, for democracy. Thus, Dahl (1971: 1) observes that "a key characteristic of a democracy is the continued responsiveness of the government to the preferences of its citizens . . ."; Riker (1982: 31) asserts that "democracy is a form of government in which the rulers are fully responsible to the ruled . . ."; while Schmitter and Karl (1991: 76) maintain that "modern political democracy is a system of governance in which rulers are held accountable for their actions in the public realm by citizens. . . ."

Yet representation is problematic. Politicians may have goals, interests, or values of their own and they may know things and undertake actions that citizens cannot observe or can monitor only at a prohibitive cost. Politicians may be willing to do anything to be (re-)elected, but they may seek private gain from holding public office or they may have some well-meaning objectives that nevertheless differ from those of citizens. If they have such motivations, they will want to do things which informed citizens would not have wanted them to do.

Prospective and Retrospective Control

Elections may induce representation in two different ways: prospective and retrospective. Prospectively, parties or candidates make policy proposals during elections and explain how these policies would affect citizens' welfare; citizens decide which of these proposals they want to be implemented. Thus, the winning platform becomes the "mandate" for the government to pursue. Retrospectively, citizens judge the incumbents for their past actions and their results, and elected politicians must anticipate these judgements if they want to remain in office.

The mandate conception of representation is widespread: scholars, journalists, and ordinary citizens rely on it as if it were axiomatic. Yet we need to ask two questions: (1) would voters always want governments to implement mandates? And (2) can they punish governments that betray them?

If both voters and politicians are perfectly informed, then politicians offer and voters vote for platforms that maximize their welfare. If exogenous conditions unfold according to anticipations, then voters want victorious politicians to adhere to the mandate. And if politicians have proposed policies which they actually prefer, they will adhere. Representation is not problematic when politicians have policy preferences, voters vote for a platform the implementation of which maximizes their welfare, and exogenous conditions do not change much.

Yet, if voters are not well informed, they cannot be sure that implementing the mandate is best for them. It is not only that people may be afraid of their own passions, but they must know that they do not know all kinds of things that governments do know. If citizens really want governments to follow their instructions, they could force them to do so. This possibility, "imperative mandate," was debated during both the American and the French constitutional debates. Yet in no existing democracy are representatives legally compelled to abide by their electoral promises. No national-level democratic constitution allows for recall. While provisions for impeachment and procedures for withdrawing confidence are common, they are never targeted at the betrayal of promises. Hence, citizens give the government some latitude to govern.

When the government announces that the conditions are not what they were anticipated to be, voters cannot be sure if implementing the mandate is still in their best interest. And if implementing the mandate is not the best the government can do, the threat of punishing incumbents who deviate from it is not credible. Voters may not like governments that betray promises, but they will not punish politicians who made them better off by deviating from them, and politicians must know that they can escape punishment for deviating from the mandate. Voters can punish politicians who betray mandates only at the time of the next election, after the effects of such a betrayal have been experienced. And since such retrospective judgements are inevitably tainted by the outcomes to which deviations from mandates have led, and by the mere passage of time, citizens cannot enforce the adherence to mandates per se. Moreover, a government may obtain a mandate from one majority but betray its supporters, hoping to be re-elected by another majority.

Yet, even if citizens are unable to control governments prospectively, they may be able to do so retrospectively. Governments are "accountable" if citizens can discern whether governments are acting in their best interest and sanction them appropriately, so that those incumbents who act in the best interest of citizens will win re-election, and those who do not will lose an election. Anticipations of retrospective judgements instill in politicians what James Madison called "an habitual recollection of their dependence on the people" (*Federalist* #57). As Alexander Hamilton (*Federalist* #72) observed:

> There are few men who would not feel . . . zeal in the discharge of a duty . . . when they were permitted to entertain a hope of obtaining by meriting, a continuance of them. This position will not be disputed as long as it is admitted that the desire of reward is one of the strongest incentives of human conduct; or that the best security for the fidelity of mankind is to make their interest coincide with their duty.

The standard explanation of how accountability induces representation relies on "retrospective voting." In this argument, citizens set some standard of performance to evaluate governments: they decide to vote for the incumbent if their income increased by at least 4 percent during the term, if streets are safe, or if the country qualifies for the World Cup. They decide to vote against the incumbent if these criteria are not fulfilled. In turn, the government, wanting to be re-elected and knowing the citizens' decision rule, does whatever possible to at least minimally satisfy these criteria.

Because governments know that citizens have only limited information about government actions and little knowledge of their consequences, they claim credit whenever things go well and disclaim responsibility when they go awry. Citizens have to somehow decide what to believe. In turn, citizens can choose whatever criteria they want to make their decisions – they are free to blame the government even for outcomes for which the incumbent is not conceivably responsible – and they can change their mind whenever they want, so that governments must be continually guessing for what they would be judged at (re-)election time. Personalities play an important role in politics because citizens often know more about individual politicians than about policies or their outcomes. Hence, they use the information about persons as a proxy for their actions in office. If governments correctly guess for what they will be judged and if citizens correctly figure out what the government is responsible for, then the mechanism works. But information is incomplete and imperfect on both sides, so this is not a likely outcome.

Moreover, we are back to the problem of multi-dimensionality. Governments pursue many policies but citizens have only one instrument to control them, the vote. One cannot control many targets with one instrument. If a government expects that it will be judged mainly by its economic performance, it can get away with unpopular cultural policies; if it expects to be evaluated mainly by its reaction to foreign threat, it can shirk in the economic realm. Even if everyone knew everything, citizens would have to choose what is important for them and governments would be able to get away with bad performance on issues of lesser importance to citizens.

The accountability mechanism does minimize gross

abuses and large mistakes by governments: it works as a "fire alarm." Yet the combined effect of limited information and multi-dimensionality is that retrospective voting is a blunt instrument for controlling governments. Neither prospective nor retrospective voting ensures that governments would be induced to promote the best interests of citizens. If people are not perfectly informed and if they are not homogeneous, governments can favor the interests of some majority (not necessarily the one that elected them) as well as their own at the expense of a minority, or even pursue their own interests or values at the expense of everyone.

Control over Bureaucracy

Most government functions, including delivery of services valued by citizens, are performed by salaried employees, not by elected politicians. Just consider the numbers: in the United States voters elect 538 representatives, the president, and the vice-president at the federal level, for the total of 540. In turn, as of March 2014, the federal government employed 2.7 million people. About half a million people occupy elected posts at state and local levels, which employ 14.3 million full-time workers. In France, voters elect 577 members of the lower chamber, 348 senators, and a president, for the total of 926, while the national government employs about 2.5 million. About 80,000 hold elected posts at the sub-national level, while the total public employment, including public hospitals, is about 5.6 million.

Controlling elected politicians is not easy, but at least the relation between them and the voters is directly mediated by elections. Citizen control over the non-elected people who exercise most of government functions, however, is indirect. Imagine that your mail is not being delivered, that teachers do not appear in school, that the police take bribes: what can you do about it? All you can do is to vote against the incumbent politicians, who are supposed to oversee the top echelons of these bureaucracies, who in turn are supposed to supervise their subordinates. This mechanism of control is thus highly indirect. With the exception of the school boards and some local police oversight bodies in the United States, our systems of representative institutions do not contain mechanisms that would aggregate individual information about the functioning of particular public bureaucracies and give it political muscle. The reason, I suspect, is historical. When representative institutions were first established, there was no public bureaucracy to speak of: the government of the United States employed 4–5,000 people, about the same as a municipality of 100,000 today. Experiments to institute mechanisms of direct control have been frequent but they repeatedly fail: when such bodies are elected, few people vote; when they are appointed, their members are co-opted by those they are supposed to supervise. This may be why people feel politically ineffective: not because voting has no causal efficacy, but because elections are a highly indirect mechanism of control over public bureaucracies.

9

Economic Performance

Much of the current dissatisfaction with elections in the developed countries is due to the stagnation of incomes of a large share of the population, and in Europe to persistently high unemployment. The consequence is an epochal change of expectations: perhaps for the first time in 200 years many people believe that their offspring will not lead better lives than they do. Moreover, at least in the United States, this belief is validated by facts: the proportion of children who at the age of 30 enjoy incomes higher than their parents had at the same age has been falling steadily and precipitously over the past five decades (Chetty et al. 2016). In the United States, for which we have the data, this decline is due more to a sharp increase in inequality rather than slower growth, while in European countries the slowdown of growth may play a larger role than increased inequality. Nevertheless, whether it is slow growth or income inequality, the erosion of the belief in intergradational progress may well be historically unprecedented and its political consequences are ominous.

Should we expect the political systems in which governments are freely elected to be better at promoting economic
development? There are good reasons to expect that elected
governments should promote economic growth:

1 Because voters care about their incomes, prices, and
employment opportunities, one can expect elected governments to pursue policies that enhance economic welfare
and to abstain from extracting excessive rents.
2 Because voters care about educational opportunities for
their children, one can expect elected governments to
foster accumulation of human capital, which in turn promotes growth.
3 Because systems in which governments are elected admit
more information into the public sphere, private investors
have information to choose better projects and governments to quickly correct their mistakes.

But there are also plausible reasons to think that elections
would hurt growth. Most importantly, several scholars maintained that because, particularly in poor countries, voters
demand immediate consumption, investment can be expected
to be lower when governments are elected. Only autocracies,
this argument goes, can repress consumption and mobilize
the massive resources necessary for the "take-off" in poor
countries.

With good reasons in favor of both sides, it may well be that
several of these arguments are true and the effects cancel each
other. It may be true, for example, that autocracies mobilize
more savings but, because their leaders are not accountable,
they extract higher rents or engage in reckless investment
projects. Or it may be true that democracies promote the
accumulation of human capital but retard the accumulation
of physical capital. To put it generally, political regimes may

affect development through different channels, some with positive and some with negative effects, so that in the end there may be little difference.

Studies examining the effect of political institutions on various aspects of economic performance tend to generate disagreements among researchers because of complicated definitional, measurement, data, and statistical issues. The central problem is that different institutions exist under different conditions, so it is difficult to distinguish the effect of exogenous conditions from the effect of institutions. Indeed, because economic outcomes in turn affect the institutions, it is not easy to detect the direction of causality. In particular, one should not be unduly impressed by the spectacular successes of China and other autocracies (South Korea before 1988; Taiwan before 1995) that grew very fast, beginning from very lower levels of income. The "growth tigers" are autocracies because poor countries grow fast once they take off and poor countries tend to be autocracies. The safest conclusion is that, on average, autocracies do not perform better economically than systems in which elections are competitive. But whether democracies grow faster or there is no difference between regimes remains unclear. When one examines the raw data, there is a small difference in favor of autocracies in the average rates of growth of the total national income. Yet because, perhaps surprisingly, democracies exhibit on average a clearly lower rate of population growth, per capita incomes grow somewhat faster in systems where governments are elected. Hence, it appears that political regimes have more impact on the demography than on the economy.

While the fastest-growing countries tend to be poor autocracies, so are the economic basket cases. In general, democracies tend to just plod along at a stable pace, while autocratic regimes differ more from each other, exhibit much higher variation during each period, and much higher variation even under the same chief executive. Explanations again abound. One claim is that free public opinion provides an "alarm" mechanism that informs democratic governments about impending disasters: this is why democracies avoid famines. Another reason may be that elected governments must obtain and maintain the support of some majority: suppose that a government has some limited amount of resources that can be allocated to three projects. In autocracies, the rulers can pick a single project which they see as most promising and allocate to it all the resources. Under democracy, different groups may have conflicting preferences about these projects and, to build a majority coalition, the government may have to divide the resources among at least two out of the three projects. Since the return to each project is uncertain, when uncertainty is lifted, autocrats either win or lose in a big way, while democrats generate more moderate gains and losses. Perhaps most importantly, elected governments cannot easily reverse many policies, particularly those that provide income security. While they can tinker with adjusting retirement payments to inflation, any drastic reduction of social expenditures is electorally suicidal. Bill Clinton is the only democratic leader who did it without suffering electoral consequences, but even Margaret Thatcher did not dare attempt it.

The autocratic volatility may explain the difference in the rates of population growth. This difference is not due to infant mortality, which is higher in autocracies, or life expectancy, which is higher in democracies, but to fertility per woman, which is higher in autocracies. The telling piece of evidence is that policies to provide old-age insurance reduce fertility in democracies but not in autocracies, which may indicate that in democracies people have confidence that, once instituted, income insurance policies will not be reversed in their lifetime, while in autocracies they fear that policies might be volatile and so hoard the safest asset they can, which is children.

The fact that democracies exhibit much lower variation of growth rates has a number of consequences. If investors are risk averse, then they should fear autocratic volatility. In particular, since policies often change significantly when autocrats change, political instability is costly to growth in autocracies. In turn, under democracy, growth rates are not affected by changes of chief executives, which are tightly regulated and routine events. Indeed, while several researchers have claimed that political instability – events such as government change, mass demonstrations, or national strikes – have a negative effect on development, this is true only of autocracies. Another important consequence is that by reducing volatility of economic policies and performance, democracy permits people to better plan their lives, including the number of children they want to have.

In the end, even if it is not clear whether systems that hold competitive elections generate faster economic growth, we do know that, at each level of economic development, democracies pay higher wages, have lower infant mortality and higher life expectancy, and lower economic volatility. The overall verdict with regard to average material welfare must be positive. Yet inequality is another matter.

10

Economic and Social Equality

Why We Can Expect Elections
to Equalize Incomes

Should we expect the political systems in which rulers are elected to generate equality in the economic and social realm? The coexistence of universal suffrage with economic inequality is hard to fathom. As we have seen, the syllogism according to which the poor would use their majority status to expropriate the rich was almost universally accepted. And it still makes sense today. Just consider the favorite argument of political economists, called the "median voter model": each individual is characterized by an endowment of labor or capital and all individuals are ranked from the richest to the poorest. Individuals vote on the rate of tax to be imposed on incomes. The revenues generated by this tax are either equally distributed to all individuals or spent on equally valued social services and public goods, so that the tax rate uniquely determines the extent of redistribution. Once the tax rate is decided, individuals decide in a decentralized way how much of their endowments, capital or labor, to supply to production. The median-voter theorem asserts that elections generate a unique collective preference for a tax rate, that this choice is the one of the voter with the median preference, and that the voter with the median preference is the one with median income. And when the distribution of incomes is right-skewed, that is, if there are more people with incomes below than above the mean income, as it is in all countries for which data exist, majority-rule should be associated with a high degree of equality of post-fisc (tax and transfer) incomes, tempered only by the economic and administrative costs of redistribution.

Yet something is wrong with this way of thinking. Two facts are startling. The first one is that the extent of income inequality does not differ much across political regimes· at every level of per capita income, the extent of inequality is not lower in democracies than in autocracies. Hence, the expectation that competitive elections would result in reducing income inequality is not fulfilled. The second fact is even more puzzling: democratic governments redistribute more income through taxes and transfers as income inequality increases from very low to intermediate levels, but they redistribute less as inequality increases once it is already high. Figure 10.1 portrays cross-national patterns, but the same pattern is found within several countries.

Explanations of why the observed rates of redistribution are lower than we would expect, of why "the poor don't take it away from the rich," come in droves. When party competition entails a dimension other than the economic one, the rate of redistribution that emerges from elections is lower than the one desired by the voter with the median income. Religion is often singled out as the second dimension, but

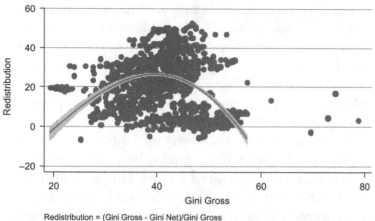

Redistribution = (Gini Gross - Gini Net)/Gini Gross
Fractional polynomial regression. Shaded area is the 95% confidence interval
Source: SWIID for economic data, CGV (2010) for democracy

Figure 10.1 *Economic inequality and redistribution under democracy*

what matters most may be the religious or ethnic divisions in a society, rather than specific religions. Some authors argue that people vote according to their norms of fairness, thinking that incomes generated by luck, say inheritance, should be redistributed, but incomes that result from hard work should not be. Other scholars believe that people vote according to their expectations of upward social mobility, opposing redistribution when they expect to become richer. Yet others maintain that the middle class is concerned about its social status and wants to preserve its distinction from the poor. Still others think that feasible redistributions are constrained by the threat of violent conflicts. Finally, surveys provide evidence that voters who hold egalitarian views often do not understand which policies would implement them. Any and all of these arguments may be true, but in my view the main culprit is that people are not politically equal in economically unequal societies.

Economic Inequality and Political Equality

While political equality is an attractive normative principle, the assumption that "the preferences of no one citizen are weighted more heavily than the preferences of any other citizen" (Dahl and Lindblom 1953: 41) cannot serve as a point of departure for analyzing the real world. Formal political equality – institutions that provide citizens with equal procedural opportunities to influence political decisions – is not sufficient to generate equality of actual influence over the outcomes because effective political influence depends on the resources that people bring to political life.

This observation was perhaps first made by Karl Marx in 1844:

> The state abolishes, in its own way, distinctions of birth, social rank, education, occupation, when it declares that birth, social rank, education, occupation, are non-political distinctions, when it proclaims, without regard to these distinctions, that every member of the nation is an equal participant in national sovereignty. ... Nevertheless the state allows private property, education, occupation to act in their way – i.e., as private property, as education, as occupation, and to exert the influence of their special nature. (Marx 1844)

When they enter the realm of politics, as citizens, individuals become anonymous. As citizens, people are not wealthy or poor, white or black, educated or illiterate, male or female. They have no qualities. But this does not mean that they have suddenly become equal. As individuals they remain wealthy or poor, educated or not. They are still endowed with unequal resources. And these resources matter for the influence they can and do exert over the policies of governments. Democracy is a universalistic system, a game with abstract, universalistic rules. But the resources that different groups bring into this game are unequal. Imagine a basketball game played between people who are seven feet tall and people who are short. The outcome is clear. When groups compete for political influence, economic power is transformed into political power, and political power in turn becomes instrumental for economic power. Organized in encompassing and centralized unions, allied with political parties, wage-earners can exert political muscles of their own, as in Scandinavia. But the political playing field is unequal in any economically unequal society.

Wealth or income affect political influence through several channels, with stronger or weaker effects on political inequality. Consider only two among several mechanisms by which differences in income may affect policy outcomes:

1 Even when they have equal rights, some people may not enjoy the material conditions necessary to participate in politics.
2 The competition among interest groups for political influence may lead policymakers to favor larger contributors.

Political inequality may emerge in economically unequal societies without anyone doing anything to enhance their influence or reduce the influence of others, simply because some people may not enjoy the material conditions necessary to exercise their political rights. Rights to act are hollow in the absence of the enabling conditions, so that the inequality of these conditions is sufficient to generate unequal political influence. While it extends to other forms of political activity, this effect of social conditions is most apparent in the fact that in most democracies poorer people tend to vote at lower rates. Empirical studies show that people with high incomes vote at rates higher than those with lower incomes whenever the salience of redistributive issues in politics or the state's extractive capacity is high. A survey conducted in 2012 in 24 European countries shows that people in the lowest-income decile voted at the rate of 69 percent, while those in the top decile voted at the rate of 85 percent. In the United States, the rates of participation were 49 percent for people with incomes under $10,000 and 81 percent for those with incomes above $150,000 in 2008 and, respectively, 47 and 80 percent in 2012.

Another reason political inequality emerges in economically unequal societies is that money can be used to influence results of elections or to influence government policies given the results of elections. Because government policies affect the welfare of groups and individuals, they want to influence these policies in their favor. To gain political influence, they are willing to incur costs that equalize at the margin (of the next dollar they spend) the benefits from the resulting policies and the costs of buying influence. In turn, governments want to remain in office while opposition parties want to occupy it. While politicians and bureaucrats may have other motivations – they may seek private rents or to maximize budgets – the inescapable fact is that politics costs money. Hence, even if all they want is to win elections, politicians may be willing to sell political influence, at least in the form of "access," but also directly in the form of policies. And because people with high incomes have more to lose from redistribution than people with low incomes can gain from it, rich people spend more money on politics.

Effective political equality is not possible in a socially and economically unequal society.

Political Inequality and Redistribution

The effect of political inequality, in turn, is that it tilts all kinds of policies in favor of people with high incomes or wealth. In particular, it reduces the rate of income redistribution compared to what would have occurred had everyone participated and had everyone had equal influence over government policies. Both the effect of social conditions on political participation and of competition for political influence on government policies vary from country to country. When left-wing parties are in office in countries which have encompassing, centralized unions, these effects seem to be small. In turn, in countries where money enters politics unabashedly and without limits, as in the United States, the effect of economic inequality is pronounced. In the most exhaustive study of the responsiveness of government policies to public opinion in the United States, Gilens (2012: 4) summarizes his findings as follows:

> What I find is hard to reconcile with the notion of political equality in Dahl's formulation of democracy. The American government does respond to the public's preferences, but that responsiveness is strongly tilted toward the most affluent citizens. Indeed, under most circumstances, the preferences of the vast majority of Americans appear to have essentially no impact on which policies the government does or doesn't adopt.

Moreover, not only is this rate generally lower but, as we have seen in Figure 10.1, above some level of income inequality redistribution decreases as inequality becomes even larger. What happens when individuals with higher incomes have greater political influence is that as income inequality

increases from low levels, the majority wants more redistribution which is still more important than the increase in the
political weight of the rich. But once income inequality is
high, so is political inequality, so that even if the majority still
wants more redistribution, people with high incomes domi-
nate politics and redistribution falls.

As a consequence of political inequality, elections have only
a limited effect on the distribution of disposable incomes,
incomes after taxes, transfers, and free social services. Hence,
contrary to all the expectations, fears and hopes, democracy
does not have much of an effect on correcting for the inequality generated by the unequal distribution of property and the
inequality generated by markets.

A Vicious Circle

Economic inequality results in political inequality; political
inequality tilts government policies in favor of people with
higher incomes. Hence, economic inequality perpetuates
itself.

This is what the data show. First, income distributions
are quite stable over time. While inequality differs greatly
across countries, it changes very little over time within each
country. Only top-income shares (those of the top 1 percent
of recipients) have been highly volatile over the long run.
Distributions of earned incomes exhibited little variation
during the twentieth century. Second, increases in inequality appear to be much more rapid than its declines. In the
United States, income inequality hovered around a constant
level until about 1970 and then increased sharply. Third,
it seems that no country rapidly equalized market incomes
without some kind of cataclysm: destruction of large property as a result of foreign occupation (the Japanese in Korea,

the Soviets in Eastern Europe), revolutions (Soviet Union), wars, or massive emigration of the poor (Norway, Sweden). The top-income shares were particularly affected by the two world wars and the Depression of 1929. In sum, it may well be that income inequality tends to increase as a result of the operation of markets – a "Newtonian" law of income distribution – unless governments actively counteract this tendency, or some cataclysmic events intervene.

11

Civil Peace

Elections as a Method of Processing Conflicts

How do we manage to process political conflicts in peace and freedom?

I anticipate that some readers may be surprised by this question. After all, we take it for granted that at some regular intervals political parties compete for office, citizens vote, some rules tell us who won and who lost, and as conflictive as the election campaign may have been, these rules are routinely obeyed. Moreover, once governments are formed, they govern in relative tranquility. Even when election results raise serious doubts, as in the United States in 2000, civil peace is maintained. Yet this is a new world. As we have seen, competitive elections in which parties peacefully alternate in office became routine only recently and only in some countries. Eruptions of violence were frequent and still continue to occur.

Here is the puzzle stripped to its bare bones. Suppose that people – whether individuals, groups, or organizations – are in conflict over some good, such as land, income, places in the university, replacement organs, or military promotions. I want it and someone else wants it; sometimes I want what is not mine. An application of some rule indicates that someone else should get it. Why would I obey this rule?

Political conflicts often concern issues other than distribution. Some conflicts arise because people have strong, often religiously motivated, views about how others should behave. Some are driven by a sheer desire for power, ambition, or vanity. Even minute issues can evoke passions: in France, for example, everyone has intense views whether members of the national soccer team should be compelled to sing "La Marseillaise" or whether 2,000 women should be permitted to wear the *burkha* in public places.

Conflicts are ubiquitous and passions at times intense. How, then, do we manage to process such conflicts in peace, without curtailing political freedom, relying on procedures and rules that indicate whose interests, values, or ambitions should prevail at a particular moment?

The very prospect that governments may change can result in a peaceful regulation of conflicts. To see this argument in its starkest form, imagine that governments are selected by a toss of a, not necessarily fair, coin: "heads" mean that the incumbents should remain in office, "tails" that they should leave. Thus, a reading of the toss designates "winners" and "losers." This designation is an instruction regarding what the winners and the losers should and should not do: the winners should move into a White or Pink House or perhaps even a palace; while there, they can take everything up to the constitutional constraint for themselves and their supporters, and they should toss the same coin again when their term is up. The losers should not move into the House and should accept getting no more than whatever they are given.

When the authorization to rule is determined by a lottery, citizens have no electoral sanction, prospective or retrospective, and incumbents have no electoral incentives to behave well while in office. Because electing governments by a lottery makes their chances of survival independent of their conduct, there are no reasons to expect that governments would act in a representative fashion because they want to earn re-election: any link between elections and representation is severed. Yet the very prospect that governments would alternate may induce the conflicting political forces to comply with the rules rather than engage in violence. Although the losers suffer temporarily by accepting the outcome of the current round, if they have a sufficient chance to win in future rounds, they may prefer to comply with the verdict of the coin toss than to revert to violence in the quest for power. Similarly, while the winners would prefer not to toss the coin again, they may be better off peacefully leaving office rather than provoking violent resistance to their usurpation of power. Examine the situation from the point of view of the losers in a particular election. They face the choice of either reverting to violence in order to grab power by force or accepting the cost of having lost and waiting to win the coin toss the next time around. What they will do depends on their chances of prevailing by force, on the cost of fighting, on the loss entailed in being governed against their will, and on their chances of winning the next time. This calculus may go either way, but they will wait, as long as the policies imposed by the winners are not too extreme or as long as their chance to win at the next opportunity is sufficiently high. In turn, the winners know that to prevent the losers from raising arms they have to moderate their policies and not abuse their incumbent advantage to deny the current losers the chance to win in the future. Regulating conflicts by a coin toss generates a situation in which peacefully waiting for one's chance may be best for each party given that the other party does the same. Bloodshed is avoided by the mere fact that the political forces expect to take turns.

Consider the presidential election in the United States in 2000. Many people, almost exactly half of those who voted, were disappointed with the outcome of this election. Yet they knew they would have a chance to win in 2004. Then came 2004 and they were even more disappointed because this time the outcome was unquestionable. Still, they hoped for 2008. And who would have expected that a society that elected and re-elected Bush and Cheney would elect Obama? It is the same expectation that makes the majority of Americans swallow Donald Trump's victory, hoping for his defeat in four years.

Yet we do not use random devices; we vote. Voting is an imposition of a will over a will. When a decision is reached by voting, some people must submit to an opinion different from theirs or to a decision contrary to their interest. Voting generates winners and losers, and it authorizes the winners to impose their will, even if within constraints, on the losers. What difference does it make that we vote? One answer to this question is that the right to vote imposes an obligation to respect the results of voting. In this view, losers obey because they see it as their duty to obey outcomes resulting from a decision process in which they voluntarily participated. Outcomes of elections are "legitimate" in the sense that people are ready to accept decisions of as yet undetermined content as long as they can participate in the making of these decisions. I do not find this view persuasive. Clearly, this is not the place to enter into a discussion of a central topic of political theory, but I stand with Kelsen (1988 [1929]: 21) when he observes that "The purely negative assumption that no individual counts more than any other does not permit to deduce the positive principle that the will of the majority should prevail."

Yet I think that voting does induce compliance, through a different mechanism. Voting constitutes "flexing muscles": a reading of chances in the eventual war. If all men are equally strong (or armed) then the distribution of votes is a proxy for the outcome of war. Clearly, once physical force diverges from sheer numbers, when the ability to wage war becomes professionalized and technical, voting no longer provides a reading of chances in a violent conflict. But voting does reveal information about passions, values, and interests. If elections are a peaceful substitute for rebellion, it is because they inform everyone who would mutiny and against what. They inform the losers – "Here is the distribution of force: if you disobey the instructions conveyed by the results of the election, I will be more likely to beat you than you will be able to beat me in a violent confrontation" and the winners – "If you do not hold elections again or if you grab too much, I will be able to put up a forbidding resistance." Elections, even those in which incumbents enjoy an overwhelming advantage, provide some information about the chances of conflicting political forces in an eventual violent resistance. When rulers (persons, parties, cliques) enter into power by force and do not hold elections, they can expect to last on average 20 years before they are removed by force; when rulers hold elections without allowing any opposition they can expect to last 25 years; in countries where elections are contested, coups and other forms of violent removal of governments occur every 46 years, while in countries where at least one peaceful alternation in power has resulted from elections they occur every 87 years. Hence, the very fact of holding elections reduces the frequency of violent conflicts, holding contested elections reduces it further, and competitive elections bring it to almost zero. Elections reduce political violence by revealing the limits to rule.

In the end, the miracle of democracy is that conflicting political forces obey the results of voting. People who have guns obey those without them. Incumbents risk their control of governmental offices by holding elections. Losers wait for their chance to win office. Conflicts are regulated, processed according to rules, and thus limited. This is not consensus, yet not mayhem either. Just regulated conflict; conflict without killing. Ballots are "paper stones."

Conditions for Peaceful Competitive Elections

This miracle does not work under all conditions. The most important condition, in order for elections to remain competitive and for their outcomes to be peacefully accepted, is that the stake in a particular election – the difference between the policies of the winner and those that would have been pursued by the loser – cannot be too low but also cannot be too high, or, when it is high, the winner of the current election must be less likely to win the subsequent one. Put differently, the more of a difference the outcome of a particular election makes, the lower must be the chance that the incumbent wins the next election. The reasoning that leads to this conclusion is intuitive: if the winner of an election fears that an electoral defeat would be disastrous for him or her personally or for his supporters, he will try everything possible not to lose by manipulating the rules, repressing the opposition, or even reverting to fraud. In turn, if the defeated opposition observes that the winner pursues policies highly damaging to its interests and values, it will be willing to wait patiently for the next election only if it expects to have a reasonable chance to win in the future and reverse the course.

If these conditions are not fulfilled, either the incumbent is tempted to maintain power by unconstitutional means or the opposition is tempted to use violence to prevent the winner from assuming office. Elections are competitive and peaceful only if the opposition expects that the winner would allow it to win in the future and the incumbent expects that if it loses the opposition will reciprocate by allowing it to return to power. Note that an important corollary of this argument is that elections cannot make much of a difference over time: either the stakes in the current election must be low or policies must be likely to be reversed in the future. Hence, the very logic of competition in which the political forces can revert to violence when they cannot tolerate the electoral outcomes implies that the extent to which elections can transform social, economic, or political conditions under which they occur in a particular society is limited.

Both high per capita income and economic equality are essential for elections to remain competitive. The reason is that any difference in economic policies between the competing parties or coalitions matters less when incomes are higher. Suppose that if your party wins an election, your income will increase by 10 percent and if it loses it will decline by 10 percent. The utility difference caused by the outcome of an election will then be smaller when your income is higher. Hence, the stakes in any election are lower in countries with higher per capita income and for groups with higher incomes within these countries.

Here is one piece of historical information. In rich countries both the winners and the losers always obey the results of elections. As Figure 11.1 shows, the probability that competitive elections would be replaced by some other way of selecting or imposing rulers converges to zero when per capita income becomes large. While about 70 democracies collapsed in poorer countries, affluent democracies have

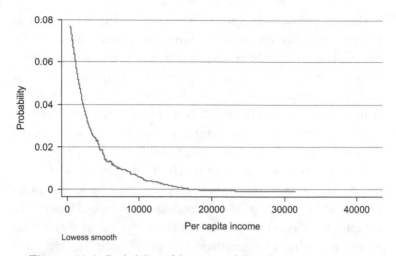

Figure 11.1 *Probability of democracy falling by per capita income*

survived wars, riots, scandals, economic and governmental crises, hell or high water.

There was an election in Costa Rica in 1948, when that country had per capita income of about $1,500. The election was technically tied: the two candidates received almost the same number of votes and there were widespread allegations of fraud, so that it was impossible to determine who in fact did win. It was not clear who should decide, but the Congress took it upon itself to declare as the winner the candidate who officially received somewhat fewer votes. A civil war ensued, in which about 3,000 people were killed. At another time, there was an election in another country. The election was technically tied: the two candidates received almost the same number of votes and there were widespread allegations of fraud, so that it was impossible to determine who in fact did win. It was not clear who should decide, but the Supreme Court, appointed in part by the father of one of the candidates, took it upon itself to declare as the winner the candidate who officially received somewhat fewer votes.

Then everyone drove home in their SUVs to cultivate their gardens. They had SUVs and gardens because this country had per capita income of about $20,000.

High income is a sufficient condition for elections to remain competitive but not a necessary one. Holding competitive elections and accepting electoral defeats is something politicians learn. Exposing oneself to the possibility of being removed from office by an election is difficult in countries that have never experienced such an event in their past, which is why 68 countries still never did. The reason is that if peaceful alternation in office by elections has never occurred in a country, the rulers cannot know what will happen if they lose. Such a situation may have occurred because no elections were held, because the opposition was prevented from competing effectively, or because voters freely kept the incumbent in office. Whatever the reasons, the prospect of defeat is a plunge into the unknown. Will the defeated incumbents survive intact, as political contenders with a prospect of some day returning to office, or will they be risking death, imprisonment, or exile, personal as well as political annihilation? Wading through untrodden waters, rulers do not know what else they would lose if they lost office, how deeply they would sink.

Yet, once an incumbent has been defeated and has yielded office peacefully, much of the uncertainty about the treatment of the defeated incumbent is lifted. The current winner now knows that the defeated party was willing to expose itself to defeat and peacefully left office when defeated. Hence, the risk facing the new incumbent is reduced. When such events – partisan alternations in office resulting from elections – are repeated, they become routine. In countries which have never experienced an alternation in their past, the probability that one would occur in the next election is only 0.12; in countries that have witnessed an alternation in a previous election this probability is already 0.30; and in countries that have experienced two alternations in the past, the probability that it would happen in the next election is 0.45, almost one election in two.

Hence, while the habit of changing governments through elections is not easy to acquire, it becomes entrenched with repeated experiences. The habit of changing rulers through elections is self-institutionalizing across institutional and economic environments. Elections peacefully process conflicts when not too much is at stake in them and when the conflicting political forces learn through experience that not too much is at stake.

12

Conclusions

Elections are a phenomenon evoking intense ambivalence. The everyday life of electoral politics is not a spectacle that inspires awe: an endless squabble among petty ambitions, rhetoric designed to hide and mislead, shady connections between power and money, laws that make no pretense of justice, policies that reinforce privilege. For better or worse, some people are dissatisfied by the incapacity of elections to make people feel that their participation is effective, some by their incapacity to assure that governments do what they are supposed to do and not do what they are not mandated to do, and many by the failure of elected governments to improve their lives. Yet some of this dissatisfaction is misplaced. Political mechanisms are embedded in societies, with their property structures, their markets, their relations of physical force, their social, ethnic, and religious divisions, their values and traditions. What any political mechanism can achieve is limited by the social conditions in which it operates. We should not expect elections to generate results that no system of choosing rulers could generate in a given society. Governments are neither ominpotent nor omniscient.

The point of departure in thinking about any method of choosing governments must be that we cannot escape being governed, and governed means being coerced to do what we may not like to do and forbidden to do what we may want to do. This much is just inescapable. Elections are the least bad mechanism of choosing our rulers because, when based on the simple-majority rule, elections minimize popular dissatisfaction with the laws by which we are governed. Rulers chosen by other mechanisms – whether heredity, co-optation, or just sheer force – can rule in ways almost no one likes, while those chosen by elections must follow the wishes of at least some majority. Still, elections inevitably generate temporary winners and losers and, while the stakes in elections cannot be too high for the mechanism to operate routinely and peacefully, finding oneself on the losing side is unpleasant. Hence, some people are always unhappy with their outcomes.

Moreover, even those who find themselves on the winning side cannot be sure that the government for which they voted would do what they wanted it to do and what it promised to do. Instructions to governments conveyed by elections are not binding because when circumstances change during the term that a government is in office, people may want governments to betray their promises. And, when conditions do change, voters cannot be certain whether the government is doing the best it can or if it is pursuing its own or someone else's interests. In turn, if they want to be re-elected, governments must anticipate how voters would judge the results of their actions by the time the next election comes. But because voters cannot be certain whether these results were due to what the government did or to circumstances beyond its control, governments can obfuscate and escape their responsibility. Hence, neither the prospective nor the retrospective mechanism of controlling governments is very effective. While particular political systems differ in the transparency of government actions, this much is again inescapable.

When we are unhappy with our lives we tend to blame politicians. In part, politicians are asking for it. Competing in elections, politicians raise expectations even when they know that there is little they can do to fulfill them. This is yet another inescapable feature of elections. Just imagine a candidate telling voters that there is nothing that can be done to remedy high unemployment, low wages, or insecure streets. Such a politician would win no votes: we want politicians to offer hope, to make promises, even when we suspect there is little they can do. But there are limits to what even the best-intentioned government can do. For one, often no one knows what it is best to do, and governments do not know either. Governments are in the unenviable situation of not having the luxury to do nothing when they do not know what to do. Even when they are not clear whether to stimulate demand or to promote fiscal discipline, they must do one of these, must act. Best economic policies, best educational policies, best welfare policies are subject to disagreements even among experts, so that when governments seek their advice, they are often told that "on the one hand, . . ." and "on the other hand, . . ."

Governments appear particularly ineffective when facing economic inequality. This impotence is partly due to the property structure of societies in which we live, societies in which decisions concerning investment and employment made by owners of productive resources affect the lives of everyone else. Capitalism imposes limits on decisions that can be reached by elections, limits that bind all governments.

Yet some of the ineffectiveness of governments in reducing economic inequality is due to the political power of those who control greater economic resources. Even when all citizens enjoy equal rights to affect government policies, their actual influence over these policies is not equal when people are economically unequal. Economic inequality generates political inequality, political inequality reproduces economic inequality: getting out of this vicious circle is difficult.

Yet governments do differ, so it is not irrational to think that some would be better than others. This is what explains the cycles of disappointment and hope. Elections incessantly rekindle our hopes. We are perennially eager to be lured by promises, to put our stakes on electoral bets. A spectator sport of mediocre quality is still thrilling and engaging. More, it is cherished, defended, and celebrated. True, those who are more dissatisfied with the functioning of democracy are less likely to see it as the best system under all circumstances. Yet many perennially hope that by organizing and participating in electoral competition they will be able to advance their values and interests.

The prospect of winning the next time around, or the one after, is what channels political actions into elections. Elections are a method by which individuals and groups, "political forces," struggle in particular societies to advance their often conflicting interests and values. They are not a mechanism which gifts us whatever we want – good government, rationality, justice, development, equality, or what not – but just a terrain on which people with heterogeneous preferences process their conflicts according to some rules. What elections generate depends, therefore, on what these actors do. But as long as the current losers have some chance to be on the winning side in the future, as long as elections are "competitive," "free," or "fair," they can wait for their turn. To process conflicts in peace, we do not have to agree: while the slogan "united we stand" may be inspiring, elections are a mechanism allowing us to stand even if divided. In the words of Bobbio (1989: 156), "What is democracy other than a set of rules . . . for the solution of conflicts without bloodshed?" This is the genius of elections.

Elections and Democracy

One thing we learned is that voting need not mean selecting, that in many elections around the world, both in the past and the present, events called "elections" do not give people a possibility of choosing governments. But are competitive elections all there is to democracy?

This is an issue about which views sharply diverge. One perspective, represented notably by Joseph Schumpeter (1942), is that governments elected by majorities should be able to govern without external constraints. The opposite view is that governments' discretion should be limited by super- or contra-majoritarian rules and institutions, such as those discussed above. The anti-majoritarian perspective is motivated by the fear that unconstrained majorities would be whimsical and despotic. In Madison's (*Federalist* #51) rendering, "If men were angels, no institutions would be necessary." Majorities cannot restraint themselves, the claim is, so that some external constraints are necessary to protect people from ill-intentioned or ill-tempered governments. Yet the counter-argument is that while limitations on majority rule may prevent governments from doing harm, they also prevent them from doing much good. Separation of powers, particularly in the form of checks and balances, disables governments from governing effectively.

My own view is pro-majoritarian, albeit with a major qualification. First, perhaps surprisingly, a theoretical argument leads to the conclusion that super-majority rule is more likely to generate despotic government than the simple-majority rule. While passing the hurdle of supra-majority – say getting a two-thirds majority in the legislature – is difficult, a government that passes the threshold of super-majority or a party that controls all the relevant institutions, the legislature, the executive, and the courts, is less afraid of losing elections and thus is free to commit excesses (Dixit, Grossman, and Gul 2000). In turn, governments supported by simple majorities restrain themselves because they fear the verdict of voters in the next election. Second, empirical evidence indicates that countries with no or few checks and balances, such as Sweden or the United Kingdom, do not exhibit sharper policy oscillations and are not more likely to violate rights than countries where governance is institutionally more divided (McGann 2006). Thus, the argument in favor of institutional limitations is unpersuasive both logically and empirically.

The qualification should be already familiar. Incumbents have many instruments to escape responsibility for their inaction as well as for actions that a majority finds offensive. Majorities can be "manufactured" by intimidating or buying the media, instrumentalizing public bureaucracies, preventing opponents from voting, and various other instruments discussed above. Hence, the crucial democratic institutions are those that prevent incumbents from abusing their power to tilt results of elections. They include administration of and oversight over elections by bodies indepenent of the executive, whether judicial or autonomous, barriers to the access of money to politics, strong enforcement of political rights: all the conditions enumerated by Dahl (1971) as necessary for elections to be truly free. The extent to which these conditions are maintained has differed across democracies during the past 60 years, so that it makes sense to speak in terms of higher or lower "quality of democracy." In the United States, in particular, the access of money to politics is almost unlimited and local administration of elections allows for abuses, often taking the form of obstacles to voting for the potential political opponents, while such practices are much less frequent in other developed democracies, say Sweden.

In the end, my view is that we should exert every effort to let the people decide freely by whom and how they want to be governed, and then let governments govern. But I certainly realize that many people think differently.

A Crisis of Democracy?

The triumph of Donald Trump in the United States, the rise of anti-establishment parties in several Western European countries, the authoritarian proclivities of some governments in Eastern Europe, notably Hungary and Poland, are seen by some observers as harbingers of an impending crisis of democracy. Results of numerous surveys showing declining support for democracy are interpreted as signs of "democratic back-sliding" or "democratic deconsolidation." There are reasons to be skeptical: crisis-mongering is a favorite form of generating sales by the media and of publicity-seeking by intellectuals. Indeed, as one looks at the titles of books published over the past 60 years, it seems that democracy has always been in crisis, that crises are, in the words of the Hungarian Marxist Georg Lukács, "just an intensification of everyday life of bourgeois society." Clearly, that a party one does not like wins an election is not a crisis of democracy. Labeling one's opponents "anti-democratic" is just a standard repertoire of politics. Yet the combination of public attitudes and the declared intentions of some political leaders may be indeed ominous.

A "crisis of democracy" may assume more or less drastic

forms: it may mean that democracy simply collapses – a democratically elected incumbent does not hold an election, or represses the opposition to the point of preventing it from winning, or the military takes power by force – or it can mean that democratic institutions are formally preserved but the political leader rules by appealing directly to "the people," ignoring institutional norms, in a form of "populism," "illiberal democracy," or whatever else one wants to call such situations. Outright collapses of democracy are relatively easy to identify, but how much and what kind of deterioration of democracy constitutes a "crisis" is an inevitably subjective assesment, so we should expect views to differ.

Consider first the easier question: what are the chances that democracy would collapse in the economically developed democracies? Contrary to frequent references to these tragic events, looking back at the advent of fascism in Europe in the 1920s and 1930s is not instructive, for the simple reason that the countries where fascism came to power were miserably poor compared to now.[2] The per capita income of Italy in 1922 was $2,631, while as of 2008 it was $19,909; of Germany, it was $3,362 in 1932 and $20,801 in 2008; of Austria, $2,940 in 1932 and $24,131 in 2008. This was just a different world. And we have seen that income is a very powerful predictor of the survival of democracies. Even ignoring the fact that democracy in this country is 200 years old, given the current income of the United States, the probability that the incumbent would not hold an election or hold one while making it impossible for the opposition to win is about 1 in 1.8 million country-years. If one believes in drawing lessons from history, an outright collapse of democracy in a country with the per capita income of the United States is just out of the realm of the imaginable. Yet history may not be a reliable

---

[2] All these numbers are in purchasing power parity 1996 dollars.

guide: some catastrophic, unprecedented events may render it mute.

In turn, inferring the stability of democracy from responses to survey questions is a publicity stunt, not a valid scientific procedure. For one, no one knows what people in different countries and at different times understand by "democracy" when they are asked whether "democracy" is the best form of government or whether it is essential that their country be governed "democratically." Even scholars argue passionately how to define "democracy," with all kinds of distinctions and qualifying adjectives: "majoritarian," "liberal," "representative," "direct," "social," even "authoritarian." And while elites see democracy in institutional terms, several surveys indicate that mass publics often conceive of it in terms of "social and economic equality." Moreover, even if recent surveys indicate that many people would want to be governed by "strong leaders" and many others by non-partisan "experts," does it mean that they do not want to have a voice in choosing the leaders or the experts? The taste for selecting governments through elections is an acquired one, but it is addictive once acquired (Przeworski 2015). Wanting governments to be effective, hoping that they will be competent and effective in improving people's lives, does not imply abdication from the right to choose them and to replace them when they fail. Finally, with all the variations in the support for democracy shown by surveys conducted in different developed countries over the past 35 years, democracy collapsed in none of them. We may be worried when few people declare confidence in political parties, parliaments, or governments, when the belief that democracy is the best system of government declines among the mass public, or when the yearning for strong leaders or the rule by experts increases. But the predictive power of answers to such questions for the outright collapse of democracy is null.

A much harder question is whether democracy will not deteriorate. Here, I think, we need to think separately about countries where the radical right is in office – the United States, Hungary, Poland – and those where it is not and is unlikely to be. The danger in the United States is the possibility that the incumbent would intimidate hostile media and create a propaganda machine of its own, that it would politicize the security agencies, that it would harass political opponents, that it would use state power to reward sympathetic private firms, that it would selectively enforce laws, that it would provoke foreign conflicts to monger fear, and that it would rig elections. Such a scenario would not be unprecedented. The United States has a long history of waves of political repression: the "red scare" of 1917–20, the internment of Japanese citizens during World War II, the McCarthy period, and the Nixon presidency. In all these cases, the Supreme Court was slow in reacting against violations of civil and political rights. Yet the Democrats lost the 1920 presidential election, Senator McCarthy was censured by the Senate, and Richard Nixon was forced to resign. In turn, the danger in the countries where the radical right would not accede to office is that governments might go too far in accommodating nativist and racist demands, and restrict civil liberties without improving the material conditions of the people most dissatisfied with the status quo.

Hence, although we should not be desperate, we should also not be sanguine. Something profound is going on. Perhaps the best diagnosis of the current situation in many democracies is "intense partisanship with weak parties."[3] Democratic elections peacefully process conflicts only when

---

[3] This diagnosis is due to a blog by Julia Azari, "Weak parties with strong partisanship are a bad combination," at <www.vox.com>, November 3, 2016.

political parties are successful in structuring conflicts and channeling political actions into elections. Representative institutions absorb conflicts only if everyone has the right to participate within these institutions, if conflicts are structured by political parties, if parties have the capacity to control their supporters, and if these organizations have the incentives to pursue their interests through the representative system. Historical experience suggests that when conflicts spill to the streets, public support for authoritarian measures designed to maintain public order tends to increase, even if street protests are targeted precisely against such authoritarian tendencies of governments. Hence, once conflicts leave institutional boundaries, they tend to escalate. Moreover, unless the opposition is united and disciplined, some groups emerge to carry on violent actions that are politically counterproductive, only providing an additional rationale for repression. When conflicts spill outside the representative framework, governments have only two choices: either to persevere with their policies while reverting to repression or to abandon policies in order to placate the opposition. Neither alternative is attractive. Spirals of breakdowns of order and repression undermine democracy, while repeated concessions to people appearing on the streets render governments unable to implement any stable policies.

My fear is that neither the government of Trump, nor Brexit, nor the governments that will be elected on the European continent will improve the everyday lives of most people, which will only strengthen the "anti-establishment" or "anti-system" sentiments. It is only natural that when people participate in successive elections, see governments change, and discover that their lives remain the same, they find something wrong with "the system" or "the establishment." Albeit extreme, Italy had 63 governments in 64 years and corruption never disappeared from the headlines. By "natural" I do not necessarily mean "rational": true, sometimes politicians are incompetent and sometimes they are corrupt, but most of the time no government can do much or knows what to do even if it wants the best.

In the end, it looks like the current crisis will simmer for the foreseeable future. Nothing much will change except for increased political polarization and increasing intensity of conflicts, at the extreme erupting from time to time in spirals of state and anti-state violence. I must admit that when I began writing this book – before Brexit, the election of Donald Trump, the failure of the Italian referendum – I did not anticipate having to close it with these speculations. We still have only limited understanding of the processes by which democracies collapse and even less of the processes by which they deteriorate. How bitter will be the lesson we are still to learn remains to be seen. In the end, it matters less who has won and who will win elections, but whether elections can still peacefully process conflicts in intensely divided societies.

Suggested Reading

Dahl, Robert A. 1971. *Polyarchy: Participation and Opposition.* New Haven: Yale University Press.

Downs, Anthony. 1957. *An Economic Theory of Democracy.* New York: Harper and Row.

Dunn, John. 2005. *Democracy: A History.* New York: Atlantic Monthly Press.

The Federalist Papers by Alexander Hamilton, James Madison and John Jay. [1788] Edited by Gary Wills. New York: Bantam Books.

Kelsen, Hans. 2013 [1929]. *The Essence and the Value of Democracy.* Edited by Nadia Urbinati and Carlo Invernizzi Accetti. Lanham: Rowman & Littlefield.

Manin, Bernard. 1997. *The Principles of Representative Government.* Cambridge: Cambridge University Press.

Morgan, Edmund S. 1988. *Inventing the People: The Rise of Popular Sovereignty in England and America.* New York: W.W. Norton.

Przeworski, Adam. 2010. *Democracy and the Limits of*

Self-Government. New York: Cambridge University Press.

Schumpeter, Joseph A. 1942. *Capitalism, Socialism, and Democracy.* New York: Harper & Brothers.

References

Arrow, Kenneth A. 1951. *Social Choice and Individual Values.*
New Haven: Yale University Press.

Bernstein, Eduard. 1961. *Evolutionary Socialism.* New York:
Schocken.

Bird, Colin. 2000. "The Possibility of Self-Government."
American Political Science Review 94: 563–77.

Black, Duncan. 1958. *The Theory of Committees and Elections.*
Cambridge: Cambridge University Press.

Bobbio, Norberto. 1989. *The Future of Democracy.*
Minneapolis: University of Minnesota Press.

Burke, Edmund. 1774. "Speech to the Electors of Bristol."
Available at: <http://oll.libertyfund.org>.

Chetty, Raj et al. 2016. "The Fading American Dream:
Trends in Absolute Income Mobility Since 1940."
Working Paper 22910. Available at: <http://www.nber.
org/papers/w22910>.

Collier, Simon and William F. Sater. 1996. *A History of Chile,
1808–1994.* Cambridge: Cambridge University Press.

Collini, Stefan, Donald Winch, and John Burrow. 1983. *That Noble Science of Politics*. Cambridge: Cambridge University Press.

Crook, Malcolm. 2002. *Elections in the French Revolution*. Cambridge: Cambridge University Press.

Cukierman, A., Edwards, S., and Tabellini, G. 1992. "Seniorage and Political Instability." *American Economic Review* 82: 537–55.

Dahl, Robert A. 1971. *Polyarchy: Participation and Opposition*. New Haven: Yale University Press.

Dahl, Robert A. and Charles E. Lindblom. 1953. *Politics, Economics, and Welfare*. New York: Harper & Brothers.

Dixit, Avinash, Gene M. Grossman, and Faruk Gul. 2000. "The Dynamics of Political Compromise." *Journal of Political Economy* 108: 531–68.

Dworkin, Ronald. 1996. *Freedom's Law*. Cambridge, MA: Harvard University Press.

The Federalist Papers by Alexander Hamilton, James Madison and John Jay. [1788] Edited by Gary Wills. New York: Bantam Books.

Foa, Roberto Stefan, and Yascha Mounk. 2016. "The Democratic Disconnect." *Journal of Democracy* 27/6: 5–17.

Gilens, Martin. 2012. *Affluence and Influence: Economic Inequality and Political Power in America*. Princeton: Princeton University Press.

Ginsburg, Tom and Mila Versteeg. 2012. "The Global Spread of Constitutional Review: An Empirical Analysis." Working paper. University of Chicago Law School.

Grossman, Gene M. and Elhanan Helpman. 2001. *Special Interest Politics*. Cambridge, MA: MIT Press.

Harding, Robin. 2011. "Freedom to Choose and Democracy: The Empirical Question." *Economics and Philosophy* 27: 221–45.

Harvey, Anna. 2015. "The Economic Origins of Entrenched

Judicial Review." *Studies in American Political Development* 29: 1–22.

Harvey, Anna. 2016. "*Buckley* v. *Valeo*, Republican Electoral Success, and Republican Polarization, 1972–1981." Working paper, Department of Politics, New York University.

Herreros, Francisco. 2005. "Screening before Sanctioning. Elections and the Republican Traditions." Working paper 05-04. Madrid: Unidad de Politicas Comparadas (CSIC).

Hofstadter, Richard. 1969. *The Idea of a Party System: The Rise of Legitimate Opposition in the United States, 1780–1840*. Berkeley: University of California Press.

Jaurès, Jean. 1971. *L'Esprit de socialisme*. Paris: Denoël.

Kelsen, Hans. 2013 [1929]. *The Essence and the Value of Democracy*. Edited by Nadia Urbinati and Carlo Invernizzi Accetti. Lanham: Rowman & Littlefield.

Lagerspetz, Eerik. 2010. "Wisdom and Numbers." *Social Science Information* 49: 29–60.

Lippmann, Walter. 1956. *The Public Philosophy*. New York: Mentor Books.

Macaulay, Thomas B. 1900. *Complete Writings*, vol. 17. Boston and New York: Houghton-Mifflin.

McGann, Anthony. 2006. *The Logic of Democracy: Reconciling Equality, Deliberation, and Minority Protection*. Ann Arbor: University of Michigan Press.

Manin, Bernard. 1997. *The Principles of Representative Government*. Cambridge: Cambridge University Press.

Marx, Karl. 1844. *On the Jewish Question*. Available at: <http://csf.colorado.edu/psn/marx/Archive/1844-JQ>.

Montesquieu. 1995 [1748]. *De l'esprit des lois*. Paris: Gallimard.

Morgan, Edmund S. 1988. *Inventing the People: The Rise of Popular Sovereignty in England and America*. New York: W.W. Norton.

Palmer, R. R. 1964. *The Age of the Democratic Revolution: vol. II. The Struggle.* Princeton: Princeton University Press.

Pasquino, Pasquale. 1998. *Sieyès et L'Invention de la Constitution en France.* Paris: Éditions Odile Jacob.

Pitkin, Hanna F. 1967. *The Concept of Representation.* Berkeley: University of California Press.

Posada-Carbó, Eduardo. 2000. "Electoral Juggling: A Comparative History of the Corruption of Suffrage in Latin America, 1830–1930." *Journal of Latin American Studies* 32: 611–44.

Prat, Andrea. 1999. "An Economic Analysis of Campaign Financing." Working paper. Columbia University. Available at: <www.columbia.edu/~ap3116/papers/WorldEconomics2.doc>.

Przeworski, Adam. 2015. "Acquiring the Habit of Changing Governments through Elections." *Comparative Political Studies* 48: 1–29.

Rae, Douglas W. 1969. "Decision Rules and Individual Values in Constitutional Choice." *American Political Science Review* 63: 40–56.

Riker, William. 1982. *Liberalism Against Populism: A Confrontation between the Theory of Democracy and the Theory of Social Choice.* San Francisco: Freeman.

Rousseau, Jean-Jacques. 1964 [1762]. *Du contrat social.* Edited by Robert Derathé. Paris: Gallimard.

Schmitt, Carl. 1993 [1928]. *Théorie de la Constitition.* Traduit de l'Allemand par Lilyane Deroche. Paris: Presses Universitaires de France.

Schmitter, Philippe, and Terry Lynn Karl. 1991. "What Democracy is . . . and What it is Not." *Journal of Democracy* 2: 75–88.

Schumpeter, Joseph A. 1942. *Capitalism, Socialism, and Democracy.* New York: Harper & Brothers.

Sharp, Andrew. 1998. *The English Levellers*. Cambridge: Cambridge University Press.

Sieyès, Emmanuel. 1970. [1789] *Qu'est-ce que le tiers état?* Edited by Roberto Zapperi. Geneva: Droz.

Simmel, Georg. 1950 [1908]. *The Sociology of Georg Simmel.* Translated, edited, and with an introduction by Kurt H. Wolff. New York: Free Press.

Wood, Gordon S. 1969. *The Creation of the American Republic, 1776–1787.* New York: W.W. Norton.